Religion in America

ADVISORY EDITOR

Edwin S. Gaustad

SERMONS AND ADDRESSES
1853-1891

Bishop Daniel A. Payne

Edited, with an Introduction by Charles Killian

ARNO PRESS

A NEW YORK TIMES COMPANY

New York • 1972

190078

Reprint Edition 1972 by Arno Press Inc.

Essay on the Education of the Ministry and
General Conference of 1852 was reprinted from
a copy in The Howard University Library
Fragments of Thought - Nos. 1 and 2 was
reprinted from a copy in The State Historical
Society of Wisconsin Library
Welcome to the Ransomed was reprinted from a
copy in The Presbyterian Historical Society
Library

RELIGION IN AMERICA - Series II
ISBN for complete set: 0-405-04050-4
See last pages of this volume for titles.

Manufactured in the United States of America

Publisher's Note: The selections in this compilation were
reprinted from the best available copies.

———————◆━●◆━◆———————

Library of Congress Cataloging in Publication Data

Payne, Daniel Alexander, Bp., 1811-1893.
    Sermons and addresses, 1853-1891.

    (Religion in America, series II)
    1. Methodist Church--Sermons. 2. Sermons,
American. I. Title.
BX8449.P3A5 1972   252.07'83   70-38458
ISBN 0-405-04079-2

Contents

INTRODUCTION

Daniel Alexander Payne used the word "providence" to explain the mosaic-like character of his career. Tragedy and adversity marched in alternation throughout his life. Born in a slave state, orphaned by ten, and denied opportunity for an education, he resolved to educate himself and to lift the spiritual, moral, and intellectual standards of his people and his church. Ascending to the bishopric of the African Methodist Episcopal Church in 1852, he served as the spiritual leader of his church longer than any man.

Payne's life covered the period from the black revolts and uprisings of the early nineteenth century to the period of Reconstruction. When blacks were leaderless, when the A. M. E. Church was struggling for survival, and when the whites were "fastening the chains of slavery and oppression" ever so tightly upon blacks, he gave direction to his people and to his church for institutional stability and racial justice.

Payne was a reformer. His reformation ideas covered three areas: spiritual, educational, and sociological. Spiritual reform was the *élan vital*. A man had to be "right" with his Creator before brotherhood could be a reality. Borrowing extensively from Wesleyan theology, he preached the kind of Gospel which suggested that the outward manifestations of reform proceeded from the changed, inner nature of man. By example and precept, he called for the spiritual revolution of man which was characterized by personalized salvation.

Payne believed that a man had to be free before he could be educated. He opposed slavery and racial injustice because freedom was basic to human nature, a nature "like unto God's." Although not as vocal as other nineteenth-century abolitionists, he fought for equality, justice, and black pride. White abolitionists praised him as an "eloquent" spokesman for the cause. Sojourner Truth and Frederick Douglass credited him for influencing their lives. In spite of his demands for spiritual and racial reform, educational reform was for him the foundation of spiritual growth and of the proper enjoyment of freedom. In 1863, when education for blacks was considered absurd and politically inexpedient, and when his own people tolerated ignorance, he purchased Wilberforce University, believing eduction to be the black man's salvation. This first venture in higher education for blacks stands as his greatest legacy.

Payne played many roles: abolitionist, educator, preacher, bishop, university president, historian, and author. In each role he attempted to influence social behavior. For him these issues were fundamental: 1) man, regardless of his color, must be free; 2) man, because of his sinful nature, must be redeemed; and 3) man, in spite of his ignorance, must be educated. In light of these possibilities, Payne's life and ministry testified to his advocacy of reform.

Payne was also a writer, carefully recording his activities in his journals and diaries. He contributed regularly to his church periodical, the *Christian Recorder.* His five editorials in the *Christian Recorder,* calling for an educated clergy, infuriated the brethren. They called him an "infidel" and a "devil," but his persistance prevailed. He often lamented that the church had no written history, so in 1848 the General Conference elected him church historian. He interrupted this project in order to finish *The Semi-Centenary and the Retrospection of the African Methodist Church* by 1866. In 1888, *The History of the A. M. E. Church* and *Domestic Education* were published.

A considerable number of Payne's sermons and essays have been lost to the public because of limited publication and poor circulation. This collection brings together many of these rare documents.

Payne gave three major speeches that indicated his position on abolition. In 1839 he spoke before the Franckean Synod of the Lutheran Church. His feelings and thoughts could be summarized on that occasion as those of a "black power" advocate of the nineteenth century. It was his most militant speech. In 1862 he spoke before a large crowd gathered to celebrate Congress' abolition of slavery in the District. His sentiments that day could be characterized as a "We Shall Overcome" speech. In 1870 he spoke before the Ohio Conference of the A. M. E. Church on the "Moral Significance of the Fifteenth Amendment." By that time his views had been tempered by theology, and the speech could have been subtitled, "God is love."

Payne's episcopal addresses were always the highlight of the General Conference. Bishop Thomas Ward, Payne's contemporary, said it was his "excellence in the pulpit" that initiated many of the improvements in the A. M. E. Church and elevated the conditions among blacks. His first episcopal address, given at Philadelphia in 1853, along with his last episcopal address given at Indianapolis in 1888, are included in this collection.

In all of Payne's preaching and writing, educational concerns within his church took first place. At the end of his presidency at Wilberforce University in 1876, he said: "Up to the present hour, God has committed no greater work to us than that of founding an institution of learning such as Wilberforce. . . . The unifying of the races is only a question of time and may the Father of humanity make Wilberforce instrumental in hastening on the glorious consummation." His favorite theme—education—was woven into all his addresses.

After Payne died in 1893, those who knew him referred to him as the black man's "Moses," an appellation he earned long before Marcus Garvey was given that title. William S. Scarborough called him the "intellectual Moses of his race." Hallie Q. Brown, one of Payne's students, likened him to Moses because he led a "mentally benighted race into intellectual freedom." The *Christian Recorder* compared him to Moses: ". . . leader and teacher, he did for us what no other did or could." Later, the *Recorder* said he was the Moses "who led his race from the Egypt of ignorance into the promised land of intelligence." Moses' trail led from Egypt to Canaan; Payne's from Charleston to the Bishopric. The volume reveals something of the "spirit" and "genius" behind that journey.

February 1972   Charles Killian

ANNUAL REPORT

AND

RETROSPECTION OF THE FIRST DECADE

OF

By Bishop D. A. PAYNE, D. D., President.

JUNE 18, 1873.

CINCINNATI:

PUBLISHED BY REV. B. W. ARNETT, PASTOR OF ALLEN TEMPLE.

Annual Report, etc.

To the Board of Trustees:

THE first decade of Wilberforce University closes with the current month. We deem it therefore proper to review the past in order that, by a careful study of its history, we may find data to calculate the probabilities of its future.

Primarily, Wilberforce University was projected in the summer of 1856, by the Cincinnati Conference of the Methodist Episcopal Church. Its Board of Trustees was organized at Xenia, Ohio, in the office of lawyer M. D. Gutch, then a Senator of the General Assembly of the State of Ohio. They were twenty-four in number, of whom four were colored men, viz.: Rev. Lewis Woodson, Mr. Ishmael Keith, of the Baptist church, Mr. Alfred Anderson, a member of the congregation of the African M. E. church at Hamilton, O., and the writer. Among the twenty whites were Governor Chase, of the State of Ohio, subsequently Secretary of the United States Treasury, and late Chief Justice of the United States.

The institution was formally dedicated to the holy work of Christian education by Rev. Edward Thompson, D. D., LL. D., then President of the Ohio Wesleyan University, and late Bishop of the M. E. Church. This dedication occurred in October, 1856. Its first principal was Rev. M. P. Gaddis, Jr., of the M. E. Church, who managed it until June, 1857. He was succeeded by Mr. I. R. Parker, an able and experienced educator of youth, assisted by his wife, as matron, and other competent teachers. His services continued till June, 1859, when he was succeeded by Rev. Richard T. Rust, D. D. Under the skillful management of the doctor the institution flourished until 1862, when the civil war drew its chief patrons into the ranks of the rebel army. These were southern planters who had sent their natural children to be educated at Wilberforce. There were at that time about one hundred students in attend-ance, among whom were about one dozen from several of the best families of the north. Among these were Rev. W. H. Hun-ter, our present book-manager, who, by the way, has thus far proven himself one of the ablest who ever had charge of our book concern; also Rev. R. H. Cain, Congressman at large of the State of South Carolina, who we hope will prove himself not only an honorable but a very efficient representative of his adopted State in the deliberations of the national congress.

President Rust was rapidly developing the institution from a primary school into a college, but inasmuch as its chief patrons at that time were slave holders, and they had entered the rebel service, its incomes were not sufficient to cover its expenditures, and, having no endowment, the Trustees were constrained, in June, 1862, to suspend operations. Thus, under the first re-gime, Wilberforce came suddenly to an end. On the 10th of March, 1863, the property was sold to the agent of the African M. E. Church, for its indebtedness, viz.: the sum of $10,000.

The land, upon which the buildings were constructed, em-braced fifty-two acres, heavily timbered; five excellent springs, impregnated with the oxide of iron, flowed in the ravine which traverses it—two of which have since been dried up, caused, I presume, by the great number of trees being cut down for fuel and other purposes.

The original college buildings were of wood, constructed nearly in the form of the letter T. The arms of the T faced the west, and were three stories high, without basement. It contained the recitation rooms, with dormitories for teachers and young ladies. The stem of the T pointed eastward, and was also of three stories, with basement, It contained the culinary apartments, a chapel one hundred by thirty feet, and dormitories for young men. The appendages to these school buildings were twelve cottages and a barn, with stables sufficient to accommodate twenty head of horses. Nine of these cottages belong to the Trustees; the other three are private property.

After contracting for this valuable and beautiful property, our first effort was to liquidate the debt. Before we could secure the title deeds, we had to pay, on the 11th of June, 1863, our first instalment of $2500. This was promptly raised by collections within the boundaries of the Baltimore and Ohio Annual Conferences. That sum was paid, and the title deed handed over to the agents of the African M. E. Church, viz. : Rev. J. A. Shorter, Rev. John G. Mitchell, and the writer; but it was particularly specified as the property of the African M. E. Church. The next step was to take out an act of incorporation. This was secured according to the laws of the State of hio. The third step was to secure a charter, which declared that two-thirds of the Board shall always be members of the A. M. E. church, and that *there shall never be any distinction among the Trustees, Faculty, or Students on account of race or color.*

Prof. John G. Mitchell was elected Principal. He was, at the time of his election, the principal of a grammar school in Cincinnati. Opening the school in the first week of July, 1863, with about one dozen children gathered from the immediate neighborhood, whose studies were elementary English, by the beginning of the following spring it grew so large that two additional teachers were needed, and Mrs. J. G. Mitchell with Miss Esther T. Maltby were chosen, the latter as Female Principal. Both she and Prof. Mitchell were graduates of Oberlin

She was a member of the Congregational Church, a fine scholar
and an earnest Christian laborer. I have seen but few young
pastors more zealous for the salvation of their flocks than was
this modest young woman for the Christian culture of the
students. Her efforts in that direction *exceeded the requirements*
of the institution. She conducted all the college prayer meetings, which were held on Monday evening, and held extra ones
every morning from 8½ to 9 o'clock, in which she always read
a portion of the word of God, and exhorted the students to
consecrate themselves to His service. Among the converts to
Christ through her ministry was that remarkably zealous young
pastor, Rev. Thomas H. Jackson, B. D., who for two years was
a professor in the theological department of Wilberforce
University; now elder in charge of the station at Columbia,
South Carolina.

Prof. Mitchell having been constrained, by the wants of the
school, to go out as a financial agent, the management of the
school was left solely to Miss Maltby, and under God it was
increasing in numbers and popularity. The progress of the
students was commendable, and classes were formed in Greek,
Latin, and the lower mathematics. Everything indicated a
prosperous future, when suddenly the buildings were set on
fire by incendiaries. Within half an hour the beautiful edifice
was nothing but smouldering embers. This catastrophe fell
upon us like a clap of thunder in a clear sky. It was a time of
lamentation for our friends and of rejoicing for our enemies.
Said one of the latter, "Now their buildings are burnt there is
no hope for them." Another had said, "I wish lightening from
heaven would burn down Wilberforce." This one supposed his
impious prayer was more than answered. But we believed and
said, "Out of the ashes of the beautiful frame building a nobler
one shall arise."

Prof. Mitchell was absent on his agency, Mrs. Mitchell had
gone to Xenia with almost all the students to witness the cele-

bration of the fall of Richmond, I was attending conference at Baltimore, and Miss Maltby was left alone. No, she was not alone. As God was with Daniel in the lions' den, and with his three brethren in the fiery furnace, so was He with her in the trouble at Wilberforce. Without faltering, one of the cottages was converted into a school-room, and the scholars taught therein till the last of June, when terminated the academic year; after which all the students from abroad went home. The majority of the advanced ones never returned, but went to other institutions. Those who preferred Wilberforce came back the next autumn.

Meanwhile we began to mature our plans for rebuilding. The result is before the country and the world. Though not completed it is a larger, finer, nobler edifice than the former. As to the school it passed through severe trials. Miss Maltby's nervous system was so affected by the catastrophe that for twelve months she was unfit for labor, and never returned. Prof. Mitchell was compelled to be in the field soliciting funds to aid us in rebuilding, and therefore, for a season, the management of the school fell upon our most advanced student, Mr. J. P. Shorter, who acted his part nobly. Prof. Mitchell of our church, Prof. Kent, an English Methodist, who had united with our church, Prof. Scoliot, a French Quaker, Miss Mary J. Woodson of our church, and Miss Josephena Jackson of the Baptist church, taught from 1866 to 1868. Profs. Fry and Adams, with Mrs. Messenger, all of the Congregational Church, taught from 1866 to 1869.

From this last date to the present, the resident teachers have been Mrs. Adams the elder, Mrs. Adams the younger, Prof. Adams, occasionally Mrs. John A. Clark, wife of the Secretary, Prof. Thomas H. Jackson, Prof. Benj. F. Lee, Miss Mary E. McBride, and Miss Emma L. Parker. Prof. Jackson left us for the work of the Christian pastorate in Columbia, South Carolina, about two months ago, and has been succeeded by Prof.

B. F. Lee. Mrs. Alice Adams was called away through the
infirmities of her aged father about three months ago, and has
been succeeded by Miss Emma L. Parker, a young lady well
qualified for the position of female principal.

Such is an outline-history of Wilberforce University under
its first regime, and such the outline view under its second.
Let us now look at

ITS PRESENT CONDITION AND RESULTS.

Its roll for the current year numbers 153, of whom 62 were
females and 91 males. The advance on last year is 27. Among
these are two Roman Catholics, two Presbyterians, two Christians, and six Baptists. The others were either professed
Methodists or of Methodist proclivities.

Our corps of resident instructors are six, of whom two are
ladies. These, with two law professors in Xenia, and four
scientific and literary lecturers from Antioch College, increase
our number to twelve. We now have five departments in the
institution, viz.: the normal and practical school, the classical,
the scientific, the law, and the theological. In the collegiate
department, which embraces the classical and scientific, there
are three seniors and three sophomores. In the academic, or
preparatory, there are three seniors and four juniors. In the
various stages of their studies are twenty-two students of theology, of whom three expect to graduate next year. In the
normal department are eighteen candidates for the teachers'
office. In the law department there is only one, and five others
preparing for it.

At the close of our first decade, we find that we have graduated four classes. In 1870, three; in 1871, one; in 1872, five;
in 1873, six; total fifteen. In addition to these we have partially educated scores of young men and women who are now
usefully employed north and south, east and west, as preachers,
teachers, and housekeepers—that is, heads of families.

Permit us here to remark that instead of having twenty-two young men preparing for the work of the Christian ministry in the A. M. E. Church, we ought to have one hundred gradu ating annually from our halls and entering the southern field. This could be easily accomplished if all the pastors in the large cities would perform their DUTY. One hundred and fifty dollars per annum can cover the expenses of a young man at Wilberforce; and it is our opinion that there is not one of the churches in our large cities (excepting the missions in them) which can not furnish that amount annually for so noble a charity, because more than twice that sum is spent annually for tobacco, and about four times that for picnics, bush meetings, and the like, notwithstanding these are the very churches that demand the best educated ministers in our several conferences. They want and demand that for which they are not willing to pay. O that there was such a wise heart in them that they could feel and know something of the good they can confer upon the connection, the race, and humanity, by educating annually some young man for the work of the Christian ministry, or some young woman to spend her energies in the work of Christian education!

WANTS OF THE SCHOOL.

The music room is needful, and ought to be finished this summer, as well for the accomplishment, which Wilberforce should impart to her students, as for the moral effect which music always exerts upon the human mind which has not been debased by ignorance or rendered stupid by superstition; and because there are now pressing demands for musical instrution. Add to these reasons the objection which many parents make to our institution because music is not taught here, and the

Trustees must both feel and see the necessity of supplying this
lack. It is also highly probable that we shall lose some of the
students we now have if this department is not opened next
autumn. The only expense which the Trustees must incur
will be the finishing of the room and putting a few chairs in
it; for, as under the old regime so under the present, the musical department will pay its own expenses. '

The more successful operations of the normal department
also demand the finishing of all the rooms on the first floor of
the south wing. We urge this upon the attention of the Trustees because of its great usefulness to the work of Christian
education among the freedmen. Demands have been made
upon us every year during the last three for experienced teachers, but no institution can send out experienced teachers unless
it has a practical school attached to it, or what may be the
equivalent of one. Moreover, the normal teacher is now the
one preferred. The power of Wilberforce will be greatly
increased, and its influence more widely diffused, if this department can be rendered perfect during the ensuing academic
year. Indeed, its practical value cannot be too highly esti-
mated, because there all the young teachers are instructed in
the science of education — in its theory, its principles, its
methods, and in their application to the school room, of whatever grade that room may be.

The basement should be completed, and at least two rooms
fitted up to accommodate such of the young women as may
prefer to do their own washing, or those whose circumstances
may compel them to do it. Such an arrangement is a consideration of economy to them personally, and of real usefulness
to the institution itself.

Lastly, efforts should be made to complete the rooms in the
Mansard roof,—and also the chapel—in order that the literary
societies and the museum may each have a place for its specific

operations; and a BETHEL consecrated to the most high, the sun and the shield of Wilberforce.

All these items are *necessities;* without them we suffer and must continue to suffer as no institution under the auspices of so large a denomination as ours ought to be allowed to suffer. These necessities should be met during the next twelve months in order that we may put Wilberforce in a commanding attitude, and set her on a more glorious career of usefulness for the second decade.

THE FUTURE.

And now, to calculate the probabilities of the future, let us look at the data before us.

The beginning of this enterprise was with nothing. When the agent of the A. M. E. Church made the purchase of the property of Wilberforce University from the assembled Trustees of the Cincinnati Conference of the M. E. Church, he had not a dollar at his command. But *he had faith in God.* It was on the night of the 10th of March, 1863, in the city of Cincinnati, O., that the proposition to sell to us was officially made. He begged for three months' time in order that he might consult the spring conferences; but no time could be given because an agent of the State of Ohio, who had been commissioned to select a place for the location of one of the asylums, and who had selected Wilberforce as the best, demanded an answer by 12 o'clock the 11th of March, in order that he might report to the legislature then in session. Therefore the Trustees said, "Now or never." Then said the agent of the A. M. E. Church: "Trusting in God, I buy the property of Wilberforce University for the African Methodist Episcopal Church." So we now have a property that many covet, and which may now be sold for $60,000, with a debt upon it of only $414.

Commencing with a primary school of about twelve children gathered from the immediate neighborhood, we have, at the end of ten years, developed it into the germ of a university, with one hundred and fifty-three students, gathered from seventeen States of the union. Within these ten years we have graduated four classes, and the one professor with whom we commenced our labors has multiplied into a corps of twelve instructors.

When we began the influence of a large majority of the surrounding country was against us. Now, to all appearances, the reverse of that is true, and our Commencement brings out some of the best citizens of the country from a distance of from five to eight miles around.

But, above all, scores of young men and women have been brought to a saving knowledge of the truth in Christ Jesus within the halls of the institution, many of whom are an ornament to the Christian profession, while a few have already entered into the "saint's everlasting rest." This statement leads us to notice what we believe to be the chief link in the chain of causes which has produced, within one decade, such valuable results.

The church of the college was organized four days after the purchase of the property, and nearly four months prior to the opening of the school. The text of the sermon preached on that occasion was Matthew xxi. 18,—"Upon this rock will I build my church, and the gates of hell shall not prevail against it." The name given it is, "The Church of the Holy Trinity." It is our conviction that from that hour God's eye and God's heart have been upon Wilberforce. As a little child stumbles and falls, sometimes through mere weakness, often through sheer carelessness or rashness, but is lifted up again and again by the hands of a wise and loving father, so have we doubtless stumbled and fallen into many errors; but the Lord, watching over us, has caused our very errors to teach us wisdom, and our blunders to make us more cautious, guarding us and leading us onward to the present point of success. And now, to confirm our faith in Himself, and in answer to many an agonizing prayer, he has sent us help from his holy hill, and succor from his tabernacle.

The latter part of my remark refers not only to the liberal donation of Chief Justice Chase, but also to all the large sums of money sent to us from time to time. They have all come from enlightened Christian sources, and from men who, knowing the inexpressible value of Christian education, are always willing to give for its support; and, Christ-like, to give not only to the strong, but more especially to the weak, in order that they may become strong, and by their strength work the more effectually for God to benefit man. In the light of these truths how heaven-sent is the bequest of the late chief justice! It came at the time of our greatest need; at the time when we all feared a syncope in the history of Wilberforce under the new regime such as occurred under the old. In view of such manifestations of the divine favor, can any one of us doubt the probable future success of Wilberforce? Can any one fail to see that God has been watching over us for good? And that He, who led Israel safely through the perils of the great howling wilderness into the possession of the promised land, will lead us through the trials of the future as He has those of the past, and set our feet upon a rock of more than a hundred thousand dollars.

THE INFERENCE.

Shall we now infer that because God has blessed us therefore we are to do nothing more? They who draw such an inference are ignorant of the demands of the Christian religion upon every one who professes it. That religion calls upon all who profess it to work, work, work, until life itself becomes extinct. Moreover, those who make such an inference have no adequate conception of the nature of a college. No! The infallible word of God teaches that the more God blesses a man the greater is the obligation of that man to give, to do, and suffer for the well-being of his fellow man. Again, what is true of the individual Christion is equally true of a denomination of Christians. The greater the manifestation of God's love to a church, the greater should be their gratitude to Him and the more intense their love for Him. But this gratitude and love is to be demonstrated by a greater outlay of energy and money for the perfection of mankind in knowledge and religion. This is to be Christ-like ; for he became poor that we might be rich, and laid down his life that every child of Adam might obtain eternal life. He who thinks otherwise is one who believes the servant to be above his master.

The true, the logical inference is, that because God has prospered the work of our hands, therefore we must work the more diligently ; because He has answered our prayers, therefore we should pray the more earnestly ; because He rewarded our faith, therefore we should be the more faithful to the trust He has committed to us. What is that trust ? The education of a denomination of Christians who are multiplying themselves into hundreds of thousands, and who, if they betrayed not their trust, if they do not trifle with it, will have more work given them by the lord of the harvest—a work which will end only with the most glorious conquests in Hayti, Africa, and many of the islands of the ocean.

Up to the present hour God has committed no greater work to us than that of founding an institution of learning such as Wilberforce promises to be ; and our success in it will depend more upon the motives which impel us, and the principles under which we manage the enterprise, than upon any other consideration. Westley-like, therefore, let us work as though we are to be saved only by works, and believe as though we are to be saved only by our faith. Then Jehovah Jirch will provide and Wilberforce become an instrument of increasing power and usefulness unto a thousand generations and unto all the races. I say unto all the races, because the Eternal has so linked every man to his fellow man, that it is impossible to educate a race without affecting for good every other race with whom it may come in contact. Moreover the unifying of the races is only a question of time, and may the Father of humanity make Wilberforce instrumental in hastening on that glorious consummation.

BISHOP PAYNE'S

FIRST ANNUAL ADDRESS

TO THE

PHILADELPHIA ANNUAL CONFERENCE

OF THE

A. M. E. CHURCH.

MAY 16, 1853.

———

PHILADELPHIA:

C. SHERMAN, PRINTER.

1853.

ANNUAL ADDRESS,

TO THE PHILADELPHIA ANNUAL CONFERENCE.

THANKS be to God the Father, God the Son, and God the Holy Spirit, through whose abundant goodness and mercy we are permitted to assemble in the Thirty-Seventh Annual Conference of the Philadelphia District.

Custom and propriety make it my duty to present you an annual address, in the opening of which permit me to hail you as brethren dearly beloved, and fellow-laborers in the common vineyard of our glorious Redeemer, who has manifested his parental care over us in the bestowment of many blessings, temporal and spiritual; also, his sovereign mercy towards the churches under our pastoral care, by the conversion of souls. In presenting my exhibit of the condition of the District, permit me to begin with

THE TEMPORAL.

CONCERNING CHURCH-BUILDING.

I am pleased to inform you that no less than four houses of worship have been finished, and dedicated to the service of the Most High, within the boundaries of the Philadelphia District. These are neat, and sufficiently commodious for the population around them. Two others are nearly finished, and will, doubtless, be consecrated within three months from the present date. I regret, however, that candor compels me to state that they have not *all* been constructed on the health-promoting principle; by which I mean to say, some are too low in their basements, others are not sufficiently ventilated. These are great physical evils, and have their origin in the ignorance of building-committees, and the indifference of the master-builders who constructed them.

I hereby solemnly protest against this mode of building, because it has been laying the foundation of disease and premature death, among both people and preachers, for the last forty years. Every basement ought to be ten feet high, at least, in the

clear, and the smallest house of worship at least sixteen feet, in the clear.   The windows in a basement
ought to be at least six feet six inches in the clear,
while the windows in the body of the church ought
to be at least nine feet six inches in the clear.
These windows should always be suspended upon
pulleys, so as to let in the air from the top of the
sash.   This will enable the preachers to speak with
more ease, and much longer, if it be needful, without danger of hoarseness, or an attack of bronchitis;
while the women and children would be less subject
to fits and fainting.

Our people should be informed of the fact that,
every time a person breathes, a gallon of air is
poisoned or corrupted; and that wherever a large
number of persons are assembled in a room, hall,
or church, this corrupted air is manufactured very
fast; and if there be no openings to carry it off, it
will lay in their bodies the foundation of disease.
that will, sooner or later, destroy their health, and
precipitate them into an untimely grave,—particularly persons who are weak in the breast, and
predisposed to consumption.

In view of this fact, who can wonder that such
gifted preachers as Joseph Corr and Thomas Woodson were cut down in the very midst of their usefulness, and at a time when the Church most needed

their talents and piety? May it not be proper to pass a resolution at this Conference, advising building-committees, who may be appointed to secure the erection of a church, to submit the details of the same to the inspection of the Bishop, who, from his extensive travels and observations, may be in possession of sufficient architectural knowledge to give judicious advice on such an important subject.

CONCERNING EDUCATION AMONG THE RISING GENERATION.

In the towns and villages we are, with few exceptions, but poorly provided. These exceptions are in favor of Norristown, Fettersville, West Chester, Burlington. and Bordentown. These schools are not only provided with teachers of respectable qualifications, but are also continued throughout the year.

Other villages have schools only six, some only three months in the year. These are the fall and winter months; the remainder of the time is spent in running about like the wild ass's colt.

Another evil existing in many schools, is that of having a male teacher during the winter, and a female in the summer. Parents seem not to know, that this perpetual change of teachers is very injurious to their children. For unless they have been

trained in the Normal schools, it is difficult to find
any two teachers whose mode is the same; so that
the habits of study inculcated by the one, are almost
always eradicated by the other. 'Tis equally true,
that it takes the greatest number of children six
months at least to become thoroughly acquainted
with the method of a teacher; in consequence of
which, they are ever learning, and never coming to
a knowledge of the truth.

Then, there are also parents who, for the most
trifling accounts, keep their children from school,
some a half day, some two or three days in each
week. Now this is also a great injury to a child's
progress in knowledge. I beseech you, brethren.
endeavor to remedy these evils.

As to the City of Philadelphia, it has, for more
than twenty years, enjoyed peculiar advantages in
this respect. During this entire period, she has had
almost always from seven to fourteen private and
three or four public schools. At present she has no
less than seven public, sixteen charity, and seventeen
private schools, making no less than forty to a population of about twenty-four thousand.

According to a recent statement made in the annual report of Mr. Benjamin Bacon, the agent for
our schools in the " City and surrounding Districts,"
there were (on the 1st of March, 1853), in the pub-

lic and charity schools, 1914 ; in the private, 325 ; making a total number of 2,329 scholars. The increased average attendance in the public schools. has been for the past year, 190 ; in the private, 44 : making a total increase of 234.

This is cheering, but yet it is not what it ought to have been. I beseech you, therefore, brethren, to put forth your energies, and make this increase more than double itself during the present year.

And this you can do by preaching on the subject once in six months at-least, and by urging the parents, in your pastoral visits, to keep their children in school. Whenever my numerous duties did allow, I have visited the schools in every village, town. and city. In Philadelphia, I have visited those private schools kept by Miss Sarah Douglass, Miss Margaretta Forten, and Miss Ada Hinton. As far as they go, they are *excellent*, and these young ladies should have the esteem and patronage due their qualifications and devotion to the intellectual and moral development of their scholars. At the head of all the institutions of learning in the Philadelphia district. stands our High School. Professor Charles Reason is the principal, assisted by Miss Grace Mapes, a young lady whose qualifications are said to be of a highly respectable character. The Professor is himself acquainted with several of the ancient and modern languages, an excellent mathematician, and well versed in polite literature. In addition to these attainments, he is one of the most accomplished teachers in the United States. In my humble judgment, it seems as if he was born for the important office of an Educator, not only on account of his peculiar fondness for it, but also because of his extraordinary aptness.

Descending himself to the root of things, he has the faculty of taking his scholars along with him, and thus making them also radical. That boy or girl must, indeed, be an incorrigible dolt, who does not learn under his training. Last Tuesday morning, I rode over the distance of twenty-seven miles to be present at his first semi-annual examination, and all who were present will justify me in the remark, that the excellent attainments of the male class demonstrate the superior abilities of their preceptor.

May I not beseech you, brethren, to urge the parents belonging to our churches to fit their children for, send them to, and keep them in the High School, until they shall have reaped the full benefit of its advantages.

RESPECTING THE DIFFUSION OF KNOWLEDGE
AMONG ADULTS.

I rejoice to state that in the city of Philadelphia
a new chapter has been opened in our history. For
in connexion with the High School, the Directors
have established a reading-room, with upwards of a
thousand volumes; this is merely the beginning.
There are funds sufficient to increase the number to
ten or twenty thousand. So we have been informed.
This library has been collected with great care, so as
to exclude the poison and chaff of light literature,
while the pure wheat of useful knowledge is plen-
teously furnished without price to every parent and
every child.

Three evenings in the week are appropriated to
the males; one afternoon to the females. Those
who do not choose to spend their leisure in the
reading-room can, under proper regulations, take
home any book they may desire, and from its con-
tents enrich their minds with the treasures of religion, of science, or philosophy.

O that the Lord would arouse our whole community to see and enjoy these advantages!

Another leaf in this opened chapter, is the attention which our people are giving to scientific lectures.
During the month of March, a lady learned in

medical science,—I mean Mrs. Oliver Johnson,—delivered two courses of lectures on Physiology and Hygiene to the ladies of our city. These lectures were well attended. In the month of April, Dr. Archibald Miles delivered another course of eight or ten lectures, on the same subject, to multitudes of both sexes. These latter lectures were kindly given by the Doctor without money or price; the happy results of which will be felt by unborn generations.

Here let me introduce that department of our affairs, which is compounded of both the temporal and spiritual, I mean

THE BOOK CONCERN.

Touching this, you will be advertised of its financial aspect through the General Book Steward and his associates. My oversight and experience have informed me of three obstacles in the way of its success, which I feel in duty bound to bring before your notice.

The first, is *the ignorance of the mass of our people.* There are thousands among us who are utterly unable to read, hence, they feel no interest in literary measures, and will, therefore, give no support to our paper or publications. A glance over the congregation of Bethel will convince you of this; for in an audience of from one to two thousand souls, you cannot see one hundred using our hymn-books.

The second obstacle *is the want of capital*.

Had we this, we could publish many works, which would be purchased by the reading community, not, indeed, on account of any regard they might have for our religious sentiments, but on account of their intrinsic literary merits; the profits of which could be applied to various benevolent purposes, such as the support of worn out ministers, the widows and orphans of those who are deceased, the publication of tracts for gratuitous distribution, and the cause of missions.

The General Conference ordained the raising of such a fund, but did not institute an efficient agency to secure the judicious measure. About the middle of last fall, I opened a subscription to aid the measure, and collected sixteen dollars, but the approaching winter caused me to desist; since then, I have not had the time to do anything in that direction. Fifty cents from each member would put the sum of $10,000 into our hands in less than three months. What church will lead off in this measure? Who will be the first to assist in this noble charity? Will it be Bethel in Philadelphia or Bethel in Baltimore?

The third obstacle *is the apathy of many in the itinerant ministry*. And you may be assured, that until every man will do his duty in relation to this matter, the affairs of the Book concern will continue to languish. It is hoped, that this Conference will do something to remove these obstacles.

———

THE SPIRITUAL.

REGARDING SUNDAY SCHOOLS.

These are generally established wherever we have societies. Some of them are tolerably conducted, others miserably. In the greater number of cases, the teachers are not qualified to unfold neither the beauties, nor sense of the word of God to the minds of the young. Some teachers attend in the morning, others in the afternoon—few attend both times; then there are others who attend both morning and afternoon, but always a half hour behind the time. These are the chief evils that retard the progress of our Sunday schools. Now, permit me to advise the remedy.

First.—Let a Bible class of the teachers be formed in every Sunday school. Let this class meet once a week for mutual instruction. Let each member of it be furnished with the following books, viz.: " The

Bible Geography," "Bible Dictionary," "Natural History of the Bible," "Nevin's Biblical Antiquities," "New Biblical Atlas," "Teacher Taught," and "The Mine Explored;" all of which can be purchased for the small sum of $4 25. Then let each school be furnished with a complete set of the maps published by the American Sunday School Union. Carefully and thoroughly studied by the teachers, these books can qualify them for an intelligent and efficient discharge of their duties. With illuminated minds, they will be able to shed such light upon the lessons of their pupils, as to make the schools places of attraction and delight; and thus, under the influences of the Holy Spirit, the Sunday school will become the garden in which plants shall be cultivated to bloom for ever amid the paradise of God.

Let exhorters be pressed into this glorious service. They tell us, that God has called them to prepare for the ministry. If so, they will be obedient, and ready to go wherever they are sent; especially if it be to take care of the tender lambs of the Redeemer's flock. If they have no heart for this, then let the Quarterly Conference take away their license; for that man who cares not for the souls of little children, was never called of God to care for the souls of old people. And let me beseech you, my dear brethren, by the mercies of God, to preach at least twice a year on the duty and necessity of family religion, in order that our children may be early taught *to love the Lord, with all their heart, and with all their soul, and with all their might.*

O that the God of Israel could say of every mother and father among us, what he said of Abraham, "I know him, that he will command his children, and his household after him, and they shall keep the way of the Lord, to do justice and judgment." *Respecting government. It is to be lamented that there is so little oneness* in the administration of discipline. In many respects we rule as though we were not of the same household. It often happens that an elder is appointed to a certain station or circuit; he is a man of incorruptible integrity, of great order, and good government; one whom money cannot bribe, nor threats deter. He will discipline the church and bring it into a prosperous condition. But his term of office expires; another elder is sent in his stead, who, from rashness and want of common sense, will undo in six months, all that his predecessor had done in two or three years.

Sometimes the difficulty will be created by the stewards, sometimes by the trustees, who will do everything which discipline enjoins, or the constitution commands, until their pride or love of power is touched; then, instead of consulting the higher, and highest authorities of the Church, they will run to a lawyer. Of course the lawyer, ever on the lookout for money, will be sure to give an opinion that has tendency and power to foster the strife; thus he fans the spark of discord into a flame, and in one week the whole congregation is set on fire. Nor can any power in or out of the Church extinguish it, until the lawsuit ends or a division takes place.

The trustees of Bethel Church in Baltimore done this very thing in 1848, which resulted in shedding the blood of one of its most gifted and faithful ministers in the very altar, and a cost of about $1,000, besides the secession of the disaffected party.

Others, who read the newspaper ten times more than their Bibles, have formed an idea that the Church must assume the same democratic or republican form as the state, and consequently be governed by similar rules; so, conceiving the resultant idea that the discipline gives the ministry too much power, they will commence a scheme of revolution, nor will they cease until the Church is rent in twain.

Now, men who will run to lawyers to find out what the discipline or article of the Church constitution means, before consulting all the authorities, and exhausting the powers of every ecclesiastical court, ought to be *immediately impeached, tried, and expelled.*

To those who would have the Church of the Living God reduced to a form corresponding to the American republic, let me say, Stop, and consider well what you are about. Do you not know that every form of government has its evil as well as its good? its disadvantages as well as its advantages? A monarchy oppresses the peasants,—the American republic oppresses and enslaves every man who has a drop of African blood in his veins, and hunts the panting fugitive like a wild beast. Now, so far as oppression and power are concerned, whether is better? It is a fact as disgraceful as it is painful, that no despot in Asia, Europe, or Africa is as cruel and relentless in the persecution of its victims as the American republic. For, not only do its politicians tell you that the black man must be oppressed and enslaved, in order that its own existence may be perpetuated; but its doctors of divinity do also declare, that " *Christianity itself has not sufficient power to make the Anglo-Saxon and the descendant of Africa live together in peace and equality.*" So then, it is a fact which no man can set aside, that the *purest democracy under Heaven is the most despotic and unrelenting* towards its victims. *The form of a government is nothing; its just laws, impartial administration, and equal freedom everything.*

To all, whether they be stewards, trustees, or pri-

2

vate members, who are ever running to lawyers for counsel against their brethren and against the authorities of the Church, I address the burning rebukes of the Apostle, "Dare any of you, having a matter against another, go to law before the unjust, and not before the saints? Do ye not know that the saints shall judge the world? and if the world shall be judged by you, are ye unworthy to judge the smallest matter? Know ye not, that we shall judge angels? how much more the things that pertain to this life? I speak to your shame. Is it so, that there is not a wise man among you? No, not one that shall be able to judge between his brethren?"

And now, let me offer some advice, respecting the Church in which we are now assembled.

According to the last parochial report, there were 1604 communicants. Now, let twelve of its principal men lead off the six hundred and four, and establish another church of our connexion, in the western, southwestern or northwestern part of the city. Let this be done as soon as a convenient place can be procured, wherein to hold the meetings. The following reasons are the grounds of my advice.

1st. The man is not living, who can discharge all the obligations which such a Church imposes.

Beside the various duties which our discipline requires an elder to perform, take the following, found
on page 111. "Family religion is wanting in many
branches, and what avails public preaching alone,
though we could preach like angels? *We must, yea,
every travelling preacher must instruct the people from
house to house.*"

Now let any elder execute this rule, in a church
as large as Bethel, and what time will be left him
for reading and study? What time for the instruction of his own wife and children?

2d. In a church as large as Bethel, there is too
much latitude for evil-doers. It is like the great
city of New York or Philadelphia, where many
thieves, robbers, and incendiaries escape, by reason
of the multitude of hiding-places. The classes also
are too large, in consequence of which, insubor-
dinate leaders have the power to do a great deal of
mischief.

3d. It is the surest method which can be adopted
to prevent another schism. The seeds of insub-
ordination are already sown in this Church, and if
my advice is not heeded, the men are now living,
who will see a more fearful and scandalous schism,
than was witnessed two or three years ago.

4th. It will do good, because it will extend the boundaries, influence, and wealth of our connexion. All other denominations act upon this principle.

There is talent now in this Church that cannot be brought into requisition, just because there is no space for its exercise; and like a pent up fire. if it is *not put out, it will burn down.*

Therefore let Bethel take my advice, and the men who are now aspiring to be leaders, exhorters, preachers, stewards, and trustees, will find ample room for the exercise of their gifts and graces.

We are now brought to view

THE EDUCATION OF THE MINISTRY.

Touching this important subject, most affectionately do I offer the following advice and reflections. As there are twenty-four hours in each day, *settle down upon the resolution to spend at least three hours every day in the cultivation of your minds.*

Let those who have not passed through the studies prescribed in discipline commence them at once, and cease not until they shall have been mastered. Let those who have passed this course ascend to the higher studies. Let them study Latin, Greek, and Hebrew.

The Latin will not only introduce you to the

learning of ancient Rome, but also make you radically familiar with your own vernacular.

The Hebrew will make you acquainted with that laconic, that poetic language, in which Moses and the prophets wrote and sung.

The Greek will make you master of that copious tongue in which Christ and the Apostles taught and preached. The study of their grammatical structure *alone*, will give to the mind *a clearness of conception, and a power of analysis,* which no other study can confer, excepting Mathematics. This will be an ample reward for all the time, labor, and money you spend in their acquisition.

Try this course for one year, and so sweet. so abundant will be the fruits, that I doubt if you will cease studying so long as you live.

" The Christian dwells, like Uriel, in the sun."

If, indeed, the private Christian dwells there. where, then, should be the abiding-place of a minister of Jesus? I answer, in that purer and brighter light of which the sun himself is but a shadow. Even the light of truth, from which all ignorance is expelled. This light is the Bible. And O, what an amount of learning, knowledge, and wisdom is required to unlock the mysteries, evolve the transcendent beauties, and appropriate the inexhaustible riches of that wondrous book, to the intellectual. moral, and religious wants of a benighted. wicked. idolatrous world! Lord Bacon, one of England's greatest philosophers, has said that "Knowledge is power," the truthfulness of which is demonstrated by England's own illustrious history.

Permit me humbly to add, that sanctified knowledge is a power at once beneficent, glorious, and tremendous. It is beneficent. because it is always delighting in good works, and conferring blessings upon mankind—it is glorious, because it shines forth with the brightness of the unclouded sun;—it is tremendous, because the man in whom it dwells is like an angel of God. armed with thunderbolts. crushing the strongholds of the empire of Satan.

We now approach the highest part of our glorious vocation, the salvation of souls in

THE REVIVALS OF RELIGION.

Truly they have not been as deep and extensive as in the years 1841–2. Yet we have abundant reason to be glad. For though the Head of the Church has not overwhelmed us with the thunderstorms of his grace, yet he has most kindly distilled upon us the evening and the morning dews of his sovereign mercy.

Yes, brethren. be glad, for angels have rejoiced in the conversion of penitent sinners during the past year throughout our circuits, and in all our stations! But cannot something be done during the opening Conference year, that will make the field still more productive?

Yes, there can be more holy living among those who bear the ark of the Lord of Hosts—more zeal and devotedness in the cause of our Redeemer—more love for the souls of perishing sinners—more tender solicitude for the reputation and usefulness of one another!

O yes! There can be found in every one of us more of the mind that was in Christ. his meekness. his gentleness, his patience. his courage, his self-denying, self-sacrificing spirit. Above all. and over all, his unspotted holiness; maintained. fortified, and rendered invulnerable by his incorruptible integrity towards God and towards man!

Then shall we be as a *shining light, yea, as a flaming fire. burning now and burning ever*. Then shall the shout of the King be heard in the camp of Israel, our conquering Immanuel will lead us on from victory to victory, and the slain of the Lord be *many*.

THE CHRISTIAN MINISTRY

Its Moral
and
Intellectual Character

Bishop Daniel A. Payne

Indianapolis
January 1859

RELIGION.

THE CHRISTIAN MINISTRY,
ITS MORAL AND INTELLECTUAL CHARACTER.

[Bishop Payne's discourse was written at the request of the Literary and Historical Society of the Missouri Conference, read before the Baltimore and Indiana, and the Missouri Conferences, and published by request of the Historical and Literary Societies of the two latter Conferences.]

" The things which thou hast heard of me among many witnesses, the same commit thou unto faithful men, who shall be able to teach others also."—2 Tim. ii. 1, 2

The teachers of mankind are manifold. There are the teachers of Law and of Medicine; of Mathematics and of Language; of Natural Philosophy, Intellectual Philosophy, and Moral Philosophy; of Chemistry and Botany; of Zoology, Mineralogy, and Geology; of History—Natural, Profane, and Ecclesiastical; of Music and of Painting.

All these are useful to mankind, and without them, the world might ultimately be reduced to barbarism. These are either self-constituted or appointed by men, and responsible to men alone for the manner in which they discharge their duties and obligations—they are called Professors.

But the teachers of religion, of its highest form, Christianity, are heaven-called, heaven-appointed, heaven-ordained. They are called *Ministers*, and responsible *first* to God; *secondarily* to Man.

It is our intention to consider the character of these latter, morally and intellectually.

I. As to their moral character, the statement of the text is this, they "must be" *faithful men.* Now faithfulness in a religious sense, and it is the only one in which the text is used, signifies not only *firmness* in our adherence to the truths of religion, but also *uprightness* and *integrity* in discharging those duties which religion enjoins upon us.

Let us analyze this *thought,* and see all the elements which enter into its composition. For if we understand the Apostle when he uses this word *faithful,* he is only putting a part for the whole; one of the most prominent traits, for all the elements of a generic term, including all the graces that constitute the Christian minister the man's character. He has also furnished the key to this analytic process, for which God be praised. Because in this, as in everything which man is permitted to touch, he has different standards of measurements, so that what is faithfulness in the estimation of one, is not faithfulness in the estimation of another.

Like temperance, one thinks he violates its precepts when he drinks a single glass of wine; another, not until he has drank a half dozen glasses; whilst a third declares that no one is drunk until he has swallowed so much liquor "that he can neither stand nor sit, lie down nor run, in a forty acre field.'' So of ministerial faithfulness, men judge differently. Thus, a Roman Catholic measures a minister's faithfulness by his implicit obedience to the Popes and the Fathers. A Presbyterian by his scrupulous attachment to the "Confession of Faith;" a Baptist by his one-sided view of baptism; a Methodist by his rigid adherence to the discipline of that church, and an Episcopalian by his love for the formula of the "Book of Common Prayer" and the doctrine of the apostolic succession.

Then, again, the balance of the scale is affected by the amount of intelligence each of these possess, respecting his distinctive creed; added to the prejudice or candor by which his mind may be colored. Here, then, we see the necessity of perpetual recurrence to the infallible word of God, for illustration as well as explanation and confirmation of its own doctrines, laws and precepts.

Doing this we shall find that what is dark in one place, may be rendered luminous in another—what is mere statement in this, is explanation in that.

Well then, in the text before us, the statement is, the ministers of Christ must be faithful men. But where is the explanation? My answer is, that the elements of it are running like veins of gold throughout the Epistles to Timothy and Titus, and are summed up in the special direction which are given Timothy for the formation of his own character, as a minister in the Church of the living God. These are contained in the 1st Epistle, 4th chap.,

12th verse, and expressed in the following words:

"Let no man despise thy youth; but be thou an example of the believers, in word, in conversation, in charity, in spirit, in faith, in purity."

The moral character of the minister of Jesus, then, must be so elevated that he will be an example of the believers.

a. *In his words.* This has reference to his speech both in the pulpit and outside of it. No foolishness, no crank sayings, no ludicrous anecdotes, no filthy comparisons, no vulgarity, no obscene epithets, no blasphemous expressions, should ever come from his lips—darkening, confusing, disgracing the text which he undertakes to expound. The doctrine, the pure doctrine—the truth, the whole truth, and nothing but the truth, should ever be his utterances, both inside and outside of the pulpit. In the sanctuary and in the parlor, the lips of the righteous *must* speak wisdom and his tongue talk of judgment, so that every word and all his words shall be "like apples of gold in pictures of silver."

The moral character of the minister of Jesus must be elevated, that he will be an example of the believer.

b. *In conversation, i. e., in conduct.* O, how careful should he walk before God and man! Rudeness in behavior disgraces the character as it lowers the dignity of the Christian ministry—so also does buffoonery, especially pulpit buffoonery, in which some men seem to pride themselves. I have seen some such men, whom people fond of fun would just as soon pay twenty-five cents to hear, as to see a clown perform in the circus.

Taking liberty with women should be also avoided, as one does a serpent, because a man can no more do this, and be sinless, than he can put his hands in the fire and escape burning.

Tippling, cigar-smoking, and tobacco-chewing, are all derogatory to the dignity of a Christian minister. As for drunkenness, what shall I say of the man who is guilty of this? The *hog pen suits* him much better than the *pulpit!* Like the adorable Saviour in all these respects, he should be a Nazerite. There is not an act which he performs in the presence of others, which will be considered apart from his ministerial character.

When a student, I was one day quite languid from excessive study, and therefore rose up to take some exercise, but as the weather was inclement, instead of going into the yard for exercise, I began to jump up and down, swinging my arms in a calesthenic manner. At this moment a little boy came into the room to supply me with fuel, and not understanding my movements, exclaimed, "Preacher dance! preacher dance! O, who ever see preacher dance!"

Let us, dear brethren, ever act at home and abroad, in private and in public, as men, conscious that the eyes of God are upon them, and that he will hold us responsible for every act, as well as every word; and who requires us to be as faithful in the former as in the latter. Because if a man's words may lead others into

error, so also his actions may lead them into hell. Moreover, a minister's moral character should *be so exalted*, that he will be an example of the believers.

c. *In charity, i. e., in love.*

In this respect his heart should be like a river, not only flowing, but widening and deepening in its onward movements — fertilizing all lands through which it passes—giving drink to every beast of the field—to all the birds of the air—conveying from shore to shore alike the heaviest and lightest burdens, and losing itself not in some quicksands or whirlpool, but in the deep ocean of Eternal Love!

To set aside figures and speak plainly, the minister of Christ should ever have his soul filled with the love of his Master, so that like him they may endure hunger and thirst, poverty and toils, reproaches and insults, persecution and death—in a word, he must have that love and that degree of it which never shrinks from the cross—giving to his soul the endurance of the ox—the meekness of the lamb —the courage of the lion—the innocence of the dove—the swiftness of the eagle—and the omnipotence of Him, whose victory was greatest when he suffered most! Yes, a minister's moral character *must be so exalted* that he will be an example of the believers.

d. *In spirit.* This idea indicates the sincerity and earnestness of his soul, as well as the meekness, gentleness and patience in which he performs all his pastoral work, and maintains the equilibrium of his character.

This gives consistency, strength, and stability to his whole being, subjectively and objectively considered. This makes him like a well-poised column in the sanctuary of the Lord, inclining neither backward nor forward—neither to the right nor the left.

Does he love his God? 'Tis not in tongue but in deed—from the depths of his heart. Does he profess love towards the brethren? He means just what he says. Does he engage in the labors of the Gospel? 'Tis not as a sluggard or an eye-servant; but as an earnest diligent laborer, who is conscious that although the toil and the pain be great, yet the reward shall be a thousand times greater. He struggles as though the glorious doctrines of the universe were dependant upon his efforts, and his *alone*. Neither censure nor praise of men can sever his heart from Christ. Pride and ambition—jealousy and malice—hatred and revenge—find no nestling place in his heart. And why? Because conscious of his own errors, infirmities and sins, he casts himself down in the dust, and cries, "Unclean! unclean!" And if at any time he be sensible of doing a virtuous action, his prayer is, "Lord, *save me from myself;*" and

> "While I draw this fleeting breath,
> Till my eyes are closed in death,
> When I rise to worlds unknown
> And behold thee on thy throne;
> Rock of Ages! cleft for me,
> Let me hide myself in thee!"

And the moral character of the Christian minister *must be so elevated* that he will be an example of the believers.

e. *In faith.* In this, as in every other quality, he must excel—believing nothing in morals, religion, or doctrine, but what God has revealed, or what can be proven by his infallible word. Such a man does not turn aside to every *humbug* or *ism*, which Satan can invent and embrace. Nay, he holds on to the doctrines of the Great Teacher, with a strong and steady hand, as the only hope for himself and for all!

Such a man will listen to the doctrines and read the fathers—but he *obeys* Christ and Christ *alone;* giving reverence to human creeds only, so far as they breathe the spirit of the written word; respecting the fathers and the doctors only, so far as they are echoes of the voice of Christ. Knowing that he has been made one of the stewards of the unsearchable riches of Christ, he will be *faithful in faith itself.*

But above all, the moral character of the Christian minister *must be so exalted*, that he will be an example of the believers.

f. *In Purity.* This virtue includes more than the idea of bodily chastity—it signifies chastity of the spirit—chastity at the very fountain-head of our thoughts, feelings, actions—it means *holiness* of the head, heart and spirit. This must be in the minister a principle as well as a sentiment, a law as well as a purpose.

It is this which makes the Almighty what he really is, not a god—but *the* God. For without holiness, he would be nothing more nor less than the greatest devil in the Universe. But covering himself with *this*, as with a garment, and constituting it the *beginning* and the *end* of his government, with all his other infinite attributes, he *is* the Great God of Moses, *glorious in holiness* as well as fearful in praises.

We repeat this idea: 'Tis not the magnitude of the sun that constitutes his glory — 'tis his dazzling light; so also, 'tis not the omnipotence of God that constitutes his glory—'tis his *immaculate holiness*. And such must be the fact in the moral character of the Christian minister. Not his talents, though they be as superior to Newton's, as his were superior to the instincts of a brute—not his learning, though that include all which men and angels yet have known—but *it is his holiness*.

Drunkenness, fornication, seduction, adultery, together with bigamy and polygamy, must be driven from his heart, as foes alike to God and man —nor can he make friendship with the men who are guilty of these crimes —because he knows that no one can touch filth without having some of it sticking to his fingers' end!

What! an adulterer, a fornicator, a seducer, a bigamist, in the sanctuary of the Lord?—as the representative—the *minister* of the Lord Jesus Christ? O, tell me ye angels! tell me, has hell a punishment meet for such a wretch?

No! The minister of Jesus cannot be guilty of such wickedness. He remembers *now*, and he remembers *ever*, that the burden of souls is laid upon his heart by the *hand* that was nailed to the cross—by the *hand* that burst asunder the bars of death and hell— by the *hand* that now wields the sceptre of the Universe—and therefore he cannot betray his trust. No! no! no! He can *never! He will be faithful even unto death.*

Like another Job, he eschews evil. Like another Paul, his conversion is in heaven. Like another Abraham, he walks before God and is perfect. O, thrice blessed is the estate of such a minister! Treading the earth, his head shall sweep the skies! Dwelling among men, he is ever now a citizen of heaven! Great, humble, earnest, holy, *faithful man*—thou art strong in the Lord and in the power of his might. Mayhap, thine eyes shall not see, nor thine ear hear, the ten thousandth part of the good which thy faithfulness shall effect. Mayhap, the Great Redeemer will hide it from thee, lest thy heart be inflated with spiritual pride, and thou fall to rise no more.

Only in the morning of the resurrection shalt thou behold the works of thy hands—the results of thine *integrity*, and then only to fill thy soul with wonder, love and praise, causing thee to cast thy crown of glory at the Redeemer's feet—crying, "Worthy is the Lamb that was slain to receive power and riches, and wisdom and strength, and honor and blessing." Verily, verily, thou *shalt walk upon the high places of the earth*—thou *shalt stand upon* Mount Zion!

II. We are now prepared to consider the intellectual character of the Christian minister.

The Apostle tells us they *shall be able to teach others*. But ,may not a man deceive himself on this point? He may — many have. There are those who mistake the *desire* to be useful for the *ability*. Now desire and ability are two distinct and independent things. A man may desire to be a king,'but this does not qualify him to wield the sceptre of a king. So also a man may desire to swim, but if he jump into a river without the ability, he will soon find himself sinking like a stone, to the bottom.

Some men, through mere desire, rush into the ministry without any qualification. They remind me of some lunatics, who fancy themselves to be kings or angels, and try to act accordingly. I remember such a man, who imagined himself a sea captain, and did walk up and down the yard with all the air of a commander, ordering one to reef in the main topsails, and another to make the soundings.

In like manner some men imagine themselves called to the work of the ministry, and desirous to engage in it, obtain recommendation from the class, license from the quarterly, and authority from the annual conference, set out booted, spurred and mounted, to do what? I ask again, to do what? You say to preach the Gospel. What Gospel? The Gospel of Christ? Well, do they? No! They preach what is in no Bible under heaven. Not even in the Alcoran of Mahomet. Rant, **obscene language, rude and vulgar ex-**

pressions. Irreverent exclamations, empty sound nonsense, and the essence of superstition, constitute the gospel they preach. So that by this kind of teaching and this kind of preaching, it has come to pass that some bearing the name of ministers, can be tiplers and drunkards; others can have two living wives, while some laymen can have four, and yet maintain their standing in the pulpit and in the church. So if you dare to speak of expelling them, others will cry out, *"Don't! don't! lest you destroy the church."*

O, Saviour, take care of thy flock! For this reason *I* " cry aloud and spare not;" *I* lift up my voice like a trumpet, showing my people their transgressions, and the *house of Levi* their sins.

For this purpose I say to you, my dear brethren, if the classes and quarterly conferences will let such men deceive them—don't you be deceived by them—let not the Annual Conferences be duped. Nay, let us examine the qualifications of every man who asks admission into the ranks of the ministry—let us try them by the discipline; yea, more: let us try them by the word of God. To this end let us see what the discipline does teach, and what the word of God commands. Hear the discipline: " Have they gifts as well as graces for the work? Have they, in some tolerable degree, a clear sound understanding, a right judgment in the things of God? A just conception of salvation by faith? And has God given them any degree of utterance? Do they speak readily, justly, clearly?" Such is the distinct, unequivocal declaration of the Discipline.

Now hear the word: "Give attendance to reading, to exhortation, to doctrine. Neglect not the gift that is in thee, which was given thee by prophecy, with the laying on of the hands of the presbytery. Meditate upon these things; give thyself wholly to them: that thy profiting may appear unto all. Take heed unto thyself, and unto the doctrine; continue in them, for in doing this, thou shalt both save thyself and them that hear thee."

Now can any one read this passage without being struck with the nervous language of the Apostle? Can any one hear it without being arrested by its earnestness? Can it be understood, without perceiving how the Holy Spirit *insists* upon a *proper and diligent exercise* of the intellect, for the purpose of improving it, by a daily, habitual, continuous contact with the *Truth*, just because *truth* is the great instrument by which God reveals himself to man, and man is made like unto God?

"Give attendance to reading. Neglect not the gift that is in thee. Mediate upon these things, give thyself wholly to them, that thy profiting may appear unto all."

All these expressions show alike the solicitude of the Eternal Spirit, and the deepness of the impression he desired to make upon the mind of Timothy; causing him, to *feel* and

know that he was not to be a *mere drone* about the hive, a snail in the garden, or a lounger about the house of God—but that he had a mind, and that mind was made for *thinking, investigating, discriminating*—for *study.*

That, therefore, a neglect of its culture would lead to disastrous consequences; that the Christian minister has no more liberty to cease from the cultivation of his mind, than the ocean has to cease its motion. Think of the disastrous consequences of the latter opposite idea, and you will see the consequences of the former opposite idea.

Let the ocean cease to move, then its waters would become as stagnant as those of a rain-barrel. Every fish in it would perish, the whole atmosphere be pregnant with pestilence, and the green earth itself struck with universal palsy, would become a field of graves!

So also with the ministers of Jesus. Let them cease to cultivate their minds by the study of holy truth, then will they retrograde back to the darkness, the superstition, and errors of heathenism, religion becomes a mere cloak of hypocrisy, blasphemy the language of its teachers, and the Church itself, like the temple at Jerusalem, once more hear the awful words, "*Let us depart, let us depart.*"

What, then, is the just inference which enlightened reason draws from the text, when it commands not only Timothy, but all the presbyters, elders, and bishops, in all countries— throughout all ages? "The things which thou hast heard of me among many witnesses, the same commit those unto faithful men, who shall be able to teach others also.'' Why, that we are ever bound to entrust the unsearchable riches of Christ, only to men who have

a. *Improvable minds.* That is, minds capable of cultivation. This lies at the foundation of all ministerial usefulness. 'Tis like the gold in the crude and flinty quartz, which needs only to pass through the crucible, in order that its intrinsic excellence may be made manifest; or the rude marble in the quarry, to pass through the plastic hands of the sculptor, in order that it may be transformed into a beautiful statute of living, active, glorious manhood.

But it is not enough that a man possess an improvable mind, he must also have

b. *An unquenchable desire for useful knowledge.*

Without this latter, the former is like a locomotive without steam— nothing but useless machinery. But if this desire is so strong that the person is content as long as he is acquiring knowledge, then; this man has in his nature another element of ability to teach others.

c. And he *must also have application.* This is essential, for if he have it not, his reading will be as seldom as it will be desultory. He will be ever learning, yet never coming to the knowledge of the truth—ever swimming on the surface, but never descending through the clear, deep waters, to the gemmed bottom of the Ocean of Science—nor rising through sublime heights of Christian philosophy to the luminous temple of revelation, and there make his dwelling-place among the angels of God.

Brother, *you* can know whether you possess this essential quality by looking at the manner in which *you* have pursued your studies. If *you* read to-day and neglect it to-morrow; if *you* study this month and omit it the next; then *you* are the very man who will never be able to teach others the deep things of the Spirit of Truth. Because you, yourself, will never reach them. And you know what a man has not, he can never give unto others.

Permit me to assure you, dear brother, that deep, clear, and solid learning is not, *cannot*, be attained by the reading of a few hours, a few months, nor a few years, but is the result of a life devoted to patient, diligent, and careful study of truth, in all its ramifications, and in all its relations.

The men to whom we commit the unsearchable riches of Christ, must also

d. Be men of *correct judgment.*

Those who teach immortal souls must have this great qualification. And inasmuch as it involves the power of comparison, it will enable him to discern the resemblance and dissimilarity between one doctrine and another—to discriminate between falsehood and truth—to scrutinize the opinions, conduct and character of men—and also trace the eternal distinctions which a wise, just, and good Creator has established between right and wrong, between good and evil, between virtue and vice.

It will also teach him how to adapt the different truths of Gospel to the varying condition and character of the children of men. For Paul does not preach at Athens, *all of the same class of truths* which he uttered at Jerusalem ; and so also his Epistles to the Hebrews differ very much from that which he addressed to the Romans.

Moreover, a correct judgment will give him ability to hold the reins of ecclesiastical government with such a hand, and to execute it in such a spirit as will save him from his pusillanimity on the one hand, and rashness on the other. And therefore, in him human passions shall neither hush the voice of Justice, nor silence the pleadings of Mercy. But these godlike attributes shall cheerfully embrace and sweetly kiss each other; when the claims of the former shall have been met by the proffers and sacrifices of the latter.

Moreover, the unsearchable riches of the Gospel must be committed only to men

e. Who have a *natural aptness* to teach others.

This is a rare qualification, as great as it is rare, and imposes upon him who possess it, a tremendous, yet glorious, responsibility. 'Tis to him in whom it dwells, what light is to the sun, so that while he is himself covered with this glorious element, he is shedding the same blessing upon all around him.

'Tis his pleasure—his happiness—to teach others, and he cannot do otherwise. He can no more keep from teaching others than the sun can refuse to shine upon all; and, like the sun, he often does it when he is not conscious of it.

The *end* of all his studies and researches into religion, science, and philosophy, *is to teach immortal souls,* and lead them to the knowledge of the truth, as it is in Christ Jesus. He does not mistake sound for sense, any more than he could mistake stones for bread, giving the people the former, just because he has not the latter. He is more anxious to make God's people intelligent and wise, than to excite their animal feelings, and make them shout. He labors, not to make them admire and praise himself, but to make them angry with themselves, fall out with their sins, and fall in love with Christ. And this he does by all plainness of speech and fitness of simile ; by arguments as strong as bars of iron; by illustrations as beautiful as the lily and the rose.

Having these five, there is one other qualification which he must not fail to possess.

f. *It is humility.* This is partly intellectual and partly moral. It is intellectual, inasmuch as its root is in a knowledge of one's self,—of one's ability,—of one's character. It is moral, inasmuch as it is a deep sense of one's own unworthiness, and comparative insignificance as a man, a scholar, and a Christian.

So that humility, instead of being incompatible with a knowledge of one's own self, is the result of that knowledge. This is the convincing or conservative principle among the graces. 'Tis to them what salt is to the meats. Without humility, talents and learning are but the accomplishments of a devil. Without humility, faith love and holiness are evanescent graces, which will quail and perish in the presence of the tempter.

This is the grace that keeps the soul down, down, down in the dust, at the very foot of the cross, causing the man to look upon himself as *nothing*, and upon Christ as *all*.

O! how sensitive is this man about his Master's honor! How solicitous for his Master's glory! How tremblingly alive to his own ignorance—his own weakness—his utter insufficiency! From the depths of his soul he is ever crying, Lord, thou knowest my weakness, be thou my strength. Thou knowest my ignorance, be thou my wisdom. Teach me, that I may not be a blind leader of the blind, but a scribe well instructed unto the Kingdom of Heaven. O! let not the people see me; let them see theé in thy vesture dipped in blood. Let them not hear me; let them hear thee in thy voice of saving truth! Like the beloved John, this man's greatest ambition is to lean his head upon the bosom of Jesus, and catch the lessons of unerring wisdom, as they fall from his sacred lips, and, therefore, *he is able to teach others also.*

Like David, he is ever conversing with nature; like Paul, he is the great student of revelation; therefore, like both, *he is able to teach others also.*

To sum all our ideas in a single sentence, *he must be holy, studious, instructive and wise.* Ever keeping his heart in contact with the Spirit of God; ever drinking from the pure fountains of truth. He teaches himself, that he may be able to teach others also.

To such a man, the Pauline injunction comes with heavenly emphasis and power, "Thou, therefore, my son, *be strong in the grace that is in Christ Jesus."*

The blacksmith must have strong muscles to wield the sledge hammer, and the soldier the broad sword; so, also, the minister of the Lord Jesus, who has to contend, not only with wicked men and women, but with principalities and powers, with spiritual wickedness in high places, he, above all men, should be strong in the grace which is in Christ Jesus.

Let the same principle of incorruptible holiness, of divine life, of self-sacrifice, which caused the Great Teacher to go about doing good, also be in thee. Let the principle be in thy soul, invigorating, and imparting to thee the strength of an angel, causing thee to fly about *doing good, and nothing but good.*

In conclusion, brethren, brethren, what now is our duty? To whom shall we commit the unsearchable riches of Christ? To drunkards, bigamists and polygamists? To drones and loungers? To men having "skulls

·that will not learn and cannot teach?
God forbid! Nay, rather let us die
than commit such a crime against
God and man. O! let that other
command of the Apostle to Timothy
be ever sounding in our ears, "Lay
hands suddenly upon no man, neither
be partaker of other men's sins; keep
thyself pure." Yes, let each one of
us *understand* this mandate, and *know
and feel* that any man who enters the
ministry without the proper qualifications, moral and intellectual, which
are indicated by the text, sins against
God; and he who helps such a man
to get into the ministry, also sins
against Him.

Whenever a young man comes forward, and tells us that he is called to
the ministry, let us examine him
rigidly, according to our excellent
discipline and the requisitions of God's
word. It is not enough that he tells
us God has called him; let him show
the evidences of his call. Some of
us are too credulous. If a man tells
us that he is called to this work, we
believe without proof; without any
qualification, we are ready to push
him into the sacred office. His say
so is not enough.

Do you not know that "fools
rush in where angels fear to tread."
He who aids a man in committing
murder is himself guilty of it. This
is true in the State, 'tis no less so in
the Church. This has been often
done. Some men have no conscience,
regard no vows, care for no responsibility which they assume, and dis-

charge no obligation they take upon
themselves.

They will *destroy* a sheep as soon
as they will *save* one.

Let us consider our Lord and Master, that great Shepherd of the sheep,
whom an inspired apostle calls the
Chief Shepherd; let us study his character, examine his matter, his manner,
and fashion ourselves according to his
lofty model. As a man, he had all
these qualifications and *more*. We do
not say that all ministers can have
them in the same degree. But this
we do maintain, that he who has them
in the largest possible degree, will be
the most successful teacher, preacher,
and shepherd.

Some men have gifts, but no graces.
Others have graces, but no gifts.
Neither of these are wanted in the
Christian ministry. I charge you,
brethren, before God and the Lord
Jesus, and the elect angels, that ye
observe these things, without prefering
one before another, doing nothing by
partiality.

Labor diligently to purify your own
hearts from sin, to enrich your own
minds with every kind of useful knowledge, to be clothed with humility as
with a garment, and thus be qualified
to teach others also.

On the Committee of Examination,
recommend no man who is not able to
teach others. In your Quarterly Conferences, so far as you have power,
suffer no man to obtain a license who
is not able to teach others.

And will you dare vote for a man
to obtain ordination, who is not able

to teach others? No, *never!* Let the whole ministry, let the whole Church pray, that the Lord Jesus may give us ministers, full of holiness, wisdom, faithfulness, "Who shall be able to teach others also." Amen, and Amen, so Lord Jesus let it be *now,* and let it be *forever.*

ESSAY
ON THE EDUCATION OF THE MINISTRY

Bishop Daniel A. Payne

Nashville 1891

ESSAY ON THE EDUCATION OF THE MINISTRY.

BY D. A. PAYNE.

The Ministers of the Gospel ought to be well educated.

We now conclude our essays by an appeal to all who are concerned, *i. e.* the whole Church. And first: We appeal to the venerable fathers of the Connection, and call upon you to assist us in this glorious enterprise by giving your sanction to our efforts. While we acknowledge that your advanced life and domestic cares may present insurmountable barriers to your improvement, we hail you as the pioneers of the Church. You, with the enterprising Richard Allen, have gone forth, the broadax of primitive labors upon your shoulders, entered the forest, hewn down the timber, and erected the stupendous fabric which now constitutes our Zion. O, cheer us, then, while we labor to beautify and array it on to perfection! Let it never be said that you were opposed to the cause of sacred learning, or that you hindered the car of improvement. But while you are descending to your peaceful and honorable graves, let us hear your invigorating voices saying unto us: "Go on, my sons, go on!" Then shall the bright pages of history hand down your memories as a precious legacy to unborn generations, who, with hearts of gratitude, shall look to this period and thank heaven that their progenitors were not the enemies, but the friends of education. Beloved young brethren, we appeal to you, because a glorious career of usefulness lies before you—an uncultivated field, long and wide, invites you to enter and drive the plowshare heavier throughout its length and breadth. Truth declares that the soil is deep and rich, and will yield an abundant harvest. Up! up! to the toil. The reward is in the fruits— your resting place is in heaven. Put forth every effort, employ every means, embrace every opportunity to cultivate your minds, and enrich them with the gems of holy learning. Be not satisfied with little things, lift your standard to the skies, and your attainments will be great. Swear eternal hatred to ignorance, and let your banner float upon the breeze of heaven with this inscription:

> Wisdom to silver we prefer,
> And gold is dross compared to her.

All difficulties then will fade away before you, and knowledge will become just what the Creator designed it to be, an element of your manhood, in which you may live and move and have your being.

Venerable mothers of Israel! we call upon you to aid us in this glorious reformation. Give us your influence; give us your money; give us your prayers. Hannah-like, dedicate your sons to the work of God before they are born; then Samuel-like, they will be heaven-called and heaven-sent, full of the spirit of wisdom, and full of grace. Teach them from their infancy to value learning more than silver and wisdom more than gold. Teach them that the glory of their manhood consists not in eating and dressing, but in the cultivation of the immortal mind and the purity of their morals. Thus will you inspire them with the love of what is great and good, paving the way to their future greatness and their future glory. O, who can sleep when earth and heaven are in motion! Who can stand aloof from a work in which the angels find delight? Who will dare to oppose that which God himself has decreed? The fall of ignorance is as certain as the fall of Babylon, and the universal spread of knowledge as the light of the Son, for the Lord hath said, "Many shall run to and fro, and knowledge shall be increased." And who does not see that this divine declaration is daily fulfilling? The press is pouring forth its millions of publications every year, in every form, and almost in every language, so that books and newspapers are becoming as common as the stones in the street. Common schools, seminaries and colleges are being erected in almost every land and every nation. Lyceums, literary societies, are being instituted among men of all ranks and all complexions, so that it may truly be said that the beaming chariot of the genius of knowledge is rolling triumphantly onward to the conquest of the world; therefore, the oppressors of education must either ground the weapons of their unequal warfare or be crushed to death beneath its ponderous wheels.

A period of light has already dawned upon the African Methodist Episcopal Church. Its morning star was seen in the doings of the General Conference of 1844; its opening glories were manifested in the decrees of the Educational Convention of 1845. Blessed is the man or woman who will aid the enterprise of heaven! Yea, thrice blessed is the one who will hasten on this age of light! In relation to this subject we can say with Moses, "O, that all the Lord's people were prophets!"

As for ourselves, we have dedicated our all to this sacred work. We have lain our souls and bodies, our time, our influence, our talents, upon the altar of our people's improvement and elevation; there we intend to bleed, and smoke, and burn, till life itself shall be extinct.

The calamitous fact that our people are entombed in ignorance and oppression forever stares us in the face; it shall be the fuel of the flames that consume us, and while we talk, and write, and pray, we shall rise above opposition and toil, cheered and inspired by that God whose lips have said, "The priest's lips should keep knowledge."

FRAGMENTS OF THOUGHT

Nos. 1 and 2

Bishop Daniel A. Payne

New York 1859

Fragments of Thought—No. 1.

BY D. A. P.

THE PSALMS.

What a sweet, what a precious book is this! 'Tis the harp, strung and tuned in heaven, which God himself has put in the hand of Man to cheer him through his earthly pilgrimage.

Is he passing through the shady glen, where, from the mountain's hollow sides, bubbling fountains pour their cooling streams? Or, does he traverse beneath the scorching sunbeams, the grassy prairie, or the sandy waste? Here, there, yonder—this harp can fill his soul with gladness, and his tongue with melting songs.

With this harp in hand, I have seen the weakest saint enter the dark valley of the shadow of death, and all the journey through; heard her sing as cheerily as the guiltless lark; seen her touching its thrilling chords, sweeter, louder, till her rapturous song seemed more like voices from the gates of heaven, than the tongue of mortal, verging into the dreary regions of the grave.

How wonderfully varied are the notes of this harp. No instrument on earth is like it. More potent than the 'Golden Shell' of Orpheus, it casts out evil spirits, and brings back from the gates of hell, souls that had been lost to innocence, virtue, and truth.

The Organ, sweet, full, varied, sublime as it is, has not the compass of this harp divine; — whose strings, whose notes, are tender as the midnight sighings of the mocking bird—and as loud, grand, sublime as the echoing thunders!

Listening to its gracious melodies, you hear now the sad moanings of the captive daughter of Judea—then the thrilling shouts of the royal victor, who, with the lion's leap, could run through a troop, and with the giant's strength, break in pieces the bow of steel.

O David! Sweet Harper of Israel! nearly thirty centuries have listened to thy matchless voice, now soft, then loud, now full of joy, then laden with grief—now pouring forth the bitter wailings of the penitent sinner, then uttering the bold, joyous anthem of the raptured saint.

Upon the mountains of Zion, and in the valleys of Judea, thy harp did first pour forth its lofty strains—now, the cloud-capped mountains and green valleys of every land, of every isle, of every nation under heaven, are vocal with the flying joys.

O that one could hear as God hears, the different languages of earth; the million tongues of her children; what music might be heard! What raptures realized! Mayhap, it would seem as though Heaven were listening to singing Earth—and Earth had been electrified by the music of Heaven!

Divine Harp! heaven-strung and heaven-attuned, the Church of God shall listen to thy sprightly carols, thy rapturous songs, thy solemn hymns, thy sublime odes, till with one mind, one heart, one tongue, all the redeemed, led on by the triumphant Saviour, shall exclaim, ' Let every thing that hath breath praise the Lord.'

And when my own blood-bought soul shall be standing upon the promontory of time, pluming her wings, clapping, stretching them for the celestial flight—then, Oh then! let me hear the harp of David sounding, sounding, still sounding in my ears, till I hear the matchless music of the heavenly harpers *sounding in Eternity!*

Fragments of Thought—No. 2.

BY D. A. P.

KNOWLEDGE AND GOLD.

Knowledge is more to be desired, and really more valuable than gold. Shall we attempt a comparison? Without the former the latter is useless. There are *now* entire regions of country where dwell myriads of immortal souls, in which, if a man should travel, with millions of gold in his possession, they would fail to secure him the common necessaries of animal life.

In those very regions, knowledge has already begun to convert the savage into a civilized man—the heathen into a meek, holy, useful Christian.

Until knowledge illumined the understanding of man, gold lay hidden in the mountain ravine, the rugged quartz and granite, or mingled with the river's sand.

Knowledge drew it forth from all these hiding places—sifting it from the sand—picking it from the ravines or wresting it from the embrace of the granite or the quartz; she converted it into circulating mediums, curious instruments, and beautiful vessels to meet the wants, the luxuries and purposes of civilized and Christian life.

Indeed, all the treasures of nature; varied in their forms, and colors as they are; countless in their number as they may be; are nothing more nor less, than materials out of which knowledge manufactures the comforts and luxuries, for which human hearts are daily sighing, and human desires daily seeking; making and marking the distinctions between savage and civilized man as broad, clear and evident as that which separates the night from the day.

In the formation of gold and its kindred treasures, God did but anticipate the desires and wants of Knowledge; and as a fond, provident father lays up good things for his children; so he hid away in the bosom of the Earth this useful metal, till his noble offspring should require it.

Give your child gold without knowledge, and this will be the self-evident proof that you wish to curse him.

Don't tell us that you have educated him as well as enriched him. For there is many an educated fool. Give him *first of all*, that *knowledge* which will *qualify* him to make a *right, proper* and *beneficent* use of gold, or give him no gold at all. 'A fool and his money soon parts,' is an old and a truthful proverb. So also, gold in the pocket of a fool is like a contagious disease in the body of a man, it *kills him* at the same time it *corrupts others.*

I admit that gold is a *great power.* But I also *contend*, that *knowledge* is a *greater.* In a country like this, where gold is an *idol* to be worshipped, who fears a ' rich negro ?'

Yet, in the same country a negro from whose intellect knowledge shines forth like sun light, is respected and cherished. In the despotic regions of the South, he is indeed a power dreadful and dreaded.

' There is gold and a multitude of rubies, but the lips of knowledge are a precious jewel.' This truth was reduced to a sentiment by the wisest monarch that ever lived. This same truth constrained the Emperor of France, to honor a negro with the splendid present of a hundred volumes, and a company of guards, to pay him a salute. So also, Louis Phillippe, the last King of the French, could embrace a colored youth and honor him with a dinner in the Royal palace, because he had made himself master of all those *forms of knowledge* embraced in the course of studies for a graduate of the University of Louis XVI. Millions of dollars of the purest gold in the coffers of an ignorant negro, could not have induced either Louis Phillippe, nor Louis Napoleon thus to do homage to manhood in the person of a ' *Black.*'

Stephen Girard, with all his gold, is but a rude piece of humanity along side of the cultivated Gerrit Smith. It is this superior knowledge which makes the difference between the two millionaires.

The former, *hog-like*, was wallowing in his gold, till death dragged him from it. The latter, *God-like*, has converted his into a stream of blessings to our common humanity, sunning all along the pathway of his generous and noble life.

Gold is but perishable dust—knowledge an indestructable power, ever increasing in force and volume as it moves onward and upward.

GENERAL CONFERENCE
OF 1852

Bishop Daniel A. Payne

Nashville 1891

GENERAL CONFERENCE OF 1852.

Opening Sermon by Rev. D. A. Payne—Bishop's Address by Bishop W. P. Quinn—Licensing Women—The Question Discussed—Election of Bishops—Rev. Willis Nazrey and Rev. D. A. Payne Elected Bishops—D. A. Payne Ordained—The Christian Herald Changed to Christian Recorder.

THE General Conference of 1852 was opened in the A. M. E. Church, in the city of New York, May 3d, about 10 A. M. It was called to order by the Rt. Rev. William Paul Quinn, and M. M. Clark, A. W. Wayman and Edward C. Africanus were the appointed secretaries. One hundred and thirty-nine persons were enrolled as members, but all were not in attendance.

Rev. D. A. Payne was called upon to preach the opening sermon, which is given below, with but two hours to prepare for the occasion:

Who is sufficient for these things?—II Cor., ii. 16.

To comprehend the meaning of the Apostle in these words, it is necessary to remember that the cause of his writing the first Epistle to Corinth was the existence of certain evils in the Church therein located, such as the dissensions growing out of a preference on the part of some for Paul, of others for Apollo, of a third class for Cephas, and of a fourth class for Christ; also the incestuous person who had married his own father's wife, and that after reproving for the first, he commanded them to cure this latter evil by excommunicating the transgressor. After rebuking their spirit of litigation, with every other prominent evil among them, he showeth them the structure of the Church of Christ, briefly alludes to the manner in which this Church is to be governed, and then closes with a graphic description of the glorious results of the death and resurrection of Christ. But in this, the second Epistle, he seems to have written for the restoration of the incestuous person, who had heartily repented of his sin, and given the proofs thereof by an utter abandonment of his evil way. He then compares the law of Moses with the glorious Gospel of Christ, showed his faithfulness and diligence in preaching it, his power as an apostle to punish obstinate sinners, and concludes with a general exhortation and prayer; from all of which it is evident that the ministry of the Gospel and Church government were the themes that fill up his vision when he exclaims in the language of the text, "Who is sufficient for these things?" Do not our hearts respond "Who is sufficient for these things?" To consider these things as clearly, and yet as briefly as possible, is our duty on this occasion, and may the Lord assist us in the important task.

(268)

First, then, the preaching of the Gospel. What do we understand by this? Various are the answers given. Some there are who believe it to consist in loud declamation and vociferous talking; some in whooping stamping and beating the bible or desk with their fists, and in cutting as many odd capers as a wild imagination can suggest; and some err so grievously on this subject as to think that he who hallooes the loudest and speaks the longest is the best preacher. Now all these crude ideas have their origin in our education, for we believe just what we have been taught. But if any man wishes to know what is preaching the Gospel, let him not ask of mere mortal man, but let him find his answer in the teachings of Him who spake as never man spake, and whose wisdom is without mixture of error. Hear him in the matchless sermon on the Mount, teaching us to find blessedness in poverty and meekness, in peace and righteousness, in mercy and purity, and to find exceeding great joy in persecution for righteousness sake. See with what divine skill he expounds the moral law, and carries its application beyond the outward and visible conduct into the interior and invisible workings of the human soul. Behold Him either in private houses or on the sea shore, or in the temple, by parables of the most striking beauty and simplicity, unfolding the great principles upon which the moral government of the universe is based, enlightening their understandings and warming their hearts with the sunbeams of eternal truth. This is preaching—preaching of the highest kind. We will do well to imitate it, in aid of which let us look for a few moments at the work of the Christian minister as a preacher of the Gospel; and

First. It is his business to make man acquainted with his relations to his God as a sinner.

To accomplish this he must re-echo the thunders of Sinai until the slumbering rebel is started into a sense of his danger, and looking into his own heart, he sees it a cage of unclean birds, or a lair of hissing serpents —the enemy of God by wicked works, and the enemy of his own soul. Listening, he hears the fearful sentence: "Cursed is every one that continueth not in everything written in the book of the law to do it." Looking below, he sees hell, as it were, moving from beneath to meet him at his coming; looking above, he beholds an indignant judge ready to pour out the vials of his wrath upon his guilty and defenseless head. Now, hear the cry of his anguished heart: "What shall I do to be saved?" The minister of the Gospel answers: "Believe in the Lord Jesus Christ, and thou shalt be saved." Immediately faith springs up in the soul of this trembling sinner, and looking to Calvary he sees there the Lamb of God who taketh away the sin of the world. With a bounding heart he exclaims, "My Lord and my God," and feels, pervading his whole being, " a peace that passeth all understanding, and a joy which is unspeakable and full of glory."

But the work of the Gospel minister stops not here—a flock of rich souls is committed to his care, and it now becomes his duty to train them for usefulness and for heaven. "But who is sufficient for these things?"

" 'Tis not a cause of small import
　　The pastor's care demands,
But what might fill an angel's heart,
　　And fill'd the Saviour's hands."

Therefore, with all possible diligence, he must feed the babes with the sincere milk of the word until they are able to eat strong meat; then he must feed them with that until they have attained the stature of a man in Christ Jesus, and teach them by all manner of good works to glorify " Our Father who is in heaven." But this does not terminate his work; still he must, with untiring diligence, arm every soldier of Christ with the panoply of God, and then lead on the sacramental host from truth to truth, from grace to grace, from victory to victory, until each of them shall have laid down his armor to take up his crown in heaven. "But who is sufficient for these things?"

And yet, the work of the Christian minister stops not here; for he is to discipline and govern the Church. This brings us to consider:

Second. A very difficult and important part of a minister's duty. Some of us believe that to discipline the Church simply means to try and expel the incorrigible. Is not this a great mistake? Is it not the very last thing the pastor should perform? Nay, dear brethren, to discipline a church implies more than this. It means to indoctrinate, to instruct, to reprove, to admonish, as well as to try and expel. You see, then, what is the pastor's duty; he is to make his flock intimately acquainted with the doctrines of the Christian Church, instruct them in the principles of Church government, reprove them for negligence and sin, admonish them of their duties and obligations, and then try and expel the obstinate, so as to keep the Church as pure as human wisdom, diligence and zeal, under divine guidance, can make it. "But who," I ask, "is sufficient for these things?"

Sufficiency is not to be found in man, but in God. Saith the apostle: " Our sufficiency is of God, who also hath made us able ministers of the New Testament; not of the letter, but of the spirit; for the letter killeth, but the spirit giveth life." Yes; our sufficiency is of God! But how is this sufficiency to be obtained? Is man a mere passive being in the matter; or does God require some action on his part? We answer, in this respect man is not like a seed placed in the ground, which can be developed by the morning and evening dews, together with the native warmth of the earth and the sunbeams. He must use the mind that God has given him; he must cultivate this mind, and seek that aid which is given to every one whom he has called to the work of the ministry.

First, then, let him cultivate his mind by all the means in his power. With the light of science, philosophy and literature, let him illumine his understanding, and carry this culture and this illumination to the highest point possible.

Secondly, then, let him seek the unction from above, the baptism of the Holy Ghost; let him live the life of faith and prayer—the life of unspotted holiness; for such was our Lord and Master Jesus Christ the

Righteous—his head was all knowledge, and his heart all holiness. He was as free from ignorance as he was free from sin. God grant that we may all seek to be like him as much in the one case as in the other. Then will we be able ministers of the New Testament, and be able with the illustrious Paul to say, "Our sufficiency is of God." Now, it is for teaching sentiments like these that I have been slandered, persecuted and hated. This has been the head and front of my offending. But brethren, am I not right? Is it not proper that I should seek the improvement of those who had not the chance of an early education? Yes; I have done it, and still will seek the improvement of all my young brethren, that they may be both intelligent, well educated and holy men. Like Moses, I can truly say: "O that all the Lord's people were prophets." Yea, indeed, I would that I was the most ignorant man among you, possessing at the same time the amount of information which God has given me, and I deem it very little compared with that which others enjoy.

But to return to the text, I ask who is sufficient to preach the Gospel of Christ, and govern the Church which he has purchased with his own blood? Who is sufficient to train this host of the Lord, and lead it on from earth to heaven? Who is sufficient to guide it through this war against principalities and powers, against spiritual wickedness in high places, against all the hosts of earth and hell, and place it triumphant upon the shining plains of glory? Who is sufficient? I answer, the man who makes Christ the model of his own Christian and ministerial character. This man, and he alone, is sufficient for these things.

After the preliminary adoption of certain rules to regulate the deliberations and the appointment of the different committees, the Rt. Rev. William Paul Quinn then delivered the Bishop's address, which of all those hitherto given is the best, and reflects credit alike upon his head and his heart. It is here presented in full:

BELOVED BRETHREN:—Another period of four years has passed since, in the providence of God, we were permitted to assemble in a similar capacity. I am happy to see on this occasion so many faces with which I am familiar; and that Providence which has spared our lives should be gratefully adored by us, and His presence supplicated for a continuance of his mercies upon us. But while we are happy in the enjoyment of again beholding the faces of each other, we should not be unmindful that death has been in our midst and has called from among us many of our fellow-laborers, among whom was our esteemed father in the Gospel, the Rt. Rev. Morris Brown. Of the piety, labors, talents and exemplary life of this good and dear man I cannot fully speak. I trust all of it is stamped upon our memory, and I also hope some able hand may hand down to posterity his name, with all his usefulness and piety. It remains with us to emulate his example, and strive like him to "do the work of an evangelist, and make full proof of our ministry," that when our work, like his, is done, we may meet him and others of our brethren in "that rest that remains to the people of God." Others have fallen whose loss we deplore, whose virtues we will cherish, and whose names we will remember with the liveliest emotions.

It is a source of heartfelt satisfaction to look over the labors of our brethren during the last four years. Our Connection has wonderfully prospered, and union and harmony to a great extent have prevailed ; our borders are enlarging, and from east, west, north and south the cheering tidings have come to us of our people flocking to the standard of truth.

Dear brethren, met, as you are, in the highest ecclesiastical court known to our Church, to promote by your legislation the temporal and spiritual welfare of our large and growing Connection, I humbly trust that in the enactment of laws for its regulation you will have an eye to the general good of the whole, and make only such as are strictly necessary, as plain, concise and perfect as human learning and intelligence can make them. In order to do this, you will have to invoke the Giver of all Good, and may his blessing rest upon you.

In my address to you four years ago I had occasion to call your attention to several things that I conceived to be of great importance to the well-being of our Church, some of which were acted upon, and some were not. To those which were not acted upon at that time I would again invite your special attention.

The first of these is the electing of another Bishop. The necessity of this must be at once plain to all without my entering into a minute detail of all the reasons that suggest such a desire upon my part; suffice it to say, that the interest of the Church in all its bearings demand it.

The second thing to which I would call your attention is the creating of the office of presiding elder. This is authorized by the Discipline, but as yet has never been carried out. The want of them, in my humble opinion, has been the cause of a great many mistakes in administering the laws, while upon the other hand all difficulties would be removed and harmony be restored to such portions of the Discipline that make provision for the office. I hope, therefore, that during your deliberations this will be carried out.

Our book concern still continues in an embarrassed condition for the want of proper and adequate support; as also the organ of the Church, which was ordered to be established at your last session. As you will be put in possession of the general book steward's report during your deliberations, I will not speak definitely on the subject, hoping, however, that you will see that the whole concern is placed on a more permanent foundation.

The Discipline of the Church will also claim a share of your deliberations, as in its present form it seems hard to be understood, and several very important alterations might with propriety be made, especially in that part relating to the ordination of elders and deacons. I would recommend a thorough revision of all the Discipline, except the doctrinal part, and so arrange it as to make it at once intelligible and easy to be understood.

I would suggest the propriety, also, of diminishing the delegation to the General Conference. As it now exists, the representation is far too large for our limited resources; and I am of the opinion that business could be facilitated, and our time of sitting would be shortened, while at the same time it could be so arranged that every department of the Church would be as generally and ably represented as now, providing the delegation was lessened. I hope that you may look upon this suggestion favorably, as in so doing you will afford great relief to the finances of the Connection, and detract nothing from its general wants or privileges.

One more subject to which I would invite your attention, and then I shall have done. The subject will, doubtless, come before you in some form or other during your session, as it occupied some of your attention during the last General Conference. It is the licensing of women in the Church. I have given the subject some thought, but not enough probably to warrant one to give an opinion in the case. All that I ask is that something distinct may be done that will be satisfactory to all, and the question be put to rest.

Should you, dear brethren, give to these different subjects that consideration and regard that they seem to require at your hands, your time and talent will be taxed to the utmost, and you will stand greatly in need of Divine help that whatever disposition is made of them, it may be done to the honor and glory of God, that when you go forth from this place you may part with mutual good will, and in the hope of a better state of things growing out of your united labors here. Let union and concession actuate you, and when the time arrives for us to take the parting hand, each one of us can go with renewed vigor and determination to battle with increased hopes of success in the vineyard of our common Master. May his Holy Spirit guide us in all our deliberations here, and when we are all done with the duties of life, bring us with peace into His presence forever.

WILLIAM PAUL QUINN.

On Friday evening, May 7th, the question of licensing women to preach, alluded to in the Bishop's address, was discussed with a great deal of judgment and spirit. Rev. Thomas Lawrence moved that license should be granted them. The motion was put and lost by a large majority.

The hour having arrived for the election of Bishops, according to a motion passed on Wednesday, all business was suspended for that purpose. Revs. Stephen Smith, J. M. Brown and E. N. Hall were appointed judges. A hymn having been sung, and a prayer offered to the Great Head of the Church that he might overrule the affairs of the Church, and especially guide the brethren in their choice, the polls were opened, and the result was the election of Rev. Willis Nazrey, of Philadelphia, Pa., a native of Virginia,

18

and D. A. Payne, of Baltimore, Md., a native of Charleston, S. C.*

On the following Thursday they were both consecrated to that responsible office by Rt. Rev. William P. Quinn, assisted by several elders.

There are powerful reasons why I should here state that while both men were elected at the same time, and Nazrey by nine more votes than Payne, the latter was the first upon whom ordination was confirmed, which established the right of seniority, because it is not mere election that constitutes a Bishop. If five or ten men were elected at the self-same moment, but one could be ordained at a time, and the first ordained is necessarily the senior of all who may be elected by the same ballot.

The third important discourse of the Conference was given upon the occasion of the ordination, by Rev. Molson M. Clark, the outlines of which we here present to the reader:

This is a true saying, if a man desire the office of a bishop, he desireth a good work.—I Timothy, chap. iii., verse 1.

The word bishop means overseer or superintendent. It was so used in the Jewish Scriptures. Joseph was an overseer or bishop in Potiphar's house. The Levites were overseers or bishops in the temple at Jerusalem. Solomon appointed many thousand overseers or bishops to oversee the work of building the temple. The apostles and primitive ministers were bishops in establishing and overseeing the Gospel Church, and our Saviour is the bishop or overseer of the souls of all men.

The idea of a bishop or overseer is seen in almost everything around us. See the busy tribes of bees in their industrial labors—they have an overseer or superintendent to direct their work. See the birds of passage, when the season to migrate to a warmer climate arrives—one takes the course and pursues the passage in front of the marshalled train, who, guided by an instinct peculiar to their nature, arrive with unerring certainty at their destined haven.

Our episcopal ordination came down to us from apostolic hands with but one small link missing out of the chain. It is known that St. Mark was a bishop of the church of Alexandria for a number of years, and after his death there was no regular succession to the time of Dionysius, a space of two hundred years. (See St. Jerome, as quoted by Bishop Hoadley in his controversy with Dr. Calamy).

---

* Four elders were put up as candidates by their friends: W. Nazrey, R. Robinson, A. R. Green and D. A. Payne. Rev. W. Nazrey was elected a Bishop by sixty-four votes; Rev. D. A. Payne was elected by fifty-five votes. Rev. R. Robinson received forty-six votes; Rev. A. R. Green, forty votes; and Revs. M. M. Clark, J. Cornish, T. Henry and William Moore each received one vote.

Here (two hundred years) is the only link wanted to make the episcopal chain entire from the Apostles down to our day. About this time, A.D. 250, Constantine the Great embraced the Christian faith and became head of the Church. He ordained Bishops, and placed them, under himself, over the churches in the various Roman provinces. These Bishops, in their annual assemblies, chose one of their number to preside. These presidents and ex-presidents constituted the Archbishops, and these Archbishops made a Pope. From the days of Constantine to the reformation in Germany, the episcopal claim was unbroken. Then, at the reformation, many of the regularly ordained Bishops passed over into the Protestant Church, and the succession came down through the Church of England. When John Wesley broke a small link from the English Church, he left episcopacy behind, and again broke the episcopal chain. Our Church being a branch from Wesley, and seeing that the chain had been broken, and desiring to weld it or mend it again, did so in the ordination of Bishop Allen, our first Bishop, for one of those who ordained him was himself ordained by Bishop White, a regularly constituted Bishop of the Protestant Episcopal Church, which never lost the regular succession. Here, then, we have the advantage of our white Methodist brethren, who cannot boast of regular episcopal succession, it having been broken by Wesley, and was not renewed till Asbury was ordained by Thomas Coke, LL.D., in the city of Baltimore, December 27th, 1784. We, therefore, can trace back the claim of episcopal succession, unbroken, to the primitive Church.

Our episcopal order commenced in the person of Rev. Richard Allen, thence down to Brown, Waters, Quinn, and to Nazrey and Payne, who are this day to be ordained. We hope to be excused if we conclude our remarks with a few extracts from the sermon delivered by Thomas Coke just before he ordained Francis Asbury, in Baltimore. He thus addressed him:

" 1. A Bishop should possess humility. This is the *preservatrix virtutum* —the garb of every other grace. As some one beautifully observes, other graces, without humility, are like a fine powder in the winds without a cover. Let a man be ever so zealous, ever so laborious, yet, if he wants humility, he will be only like Penelope with her web, in the ancient fable, undoing at one time what she does at another.

"2. He should have meekness. This is a passive grace which flows out in the converse and the carriage. It is certain courtesy. Grace is poured into his lips, for out of the fullness of the Lord he receiveth grace for grace.

"3. His patience. This is the grace that 'endures all things,' that flows out in sufferings and trials, and bears up the soul under every difficulty; *sub pondere crescit.* The more it is exercised, the stronger it grows.

"4. His impartiality. This is the rarest of all virtues, and yet one of the most important for a ruler of the Church. There is nothing more intolerable to mankind than partiality in him that governs, and it always springs, in part, from a meanness and a baseness of mind. It always meets with resistance from the governed. But the Christian Bishop is without partiality and without hypocrisy.

"5. His wisdom. This reigns over all his soul. He is prepared for it by the God of nature, and endowed with it by the God of grace. He was born to govern.

"Finally, Oh thou man of God, follow after righteousness, godliness, faith, love, patience and meekness. Be thou an example to the believers, in word, in conversation, in charity, in spirit, in faith, in purity. Keep that which is committed to thy trust."

Oh thou who art the Holy one of Israel, consecrate these, thy servants, with the fire of divine love; separate them for the most glorious purposes; make them stars in thy right hand, and fulfill in them and by them all the good pleasure of thy goodness. Amen.

This discourse of Brother Clark was uttered in a power and with a melting unction that bathed the audience in tears.

During the progress of our deliberations, certain distinguished divines of other denomiaations visited us, and were introduced to the General Conference. Among these were Dr. Pennington, of the Presbyterian Church, N. S.; Dr. Thompson, of the M. E. Church, president of the Ohio Wesleyan University; and Rev. Charles Avery, founder of Avery College, Allegheny, Pa. The last named gentleman, having been introduced to the Conference by Rev. Stephen Smith, rose and said that he felt grateful to God for the privilege he enjoyed of speaking in the presence of the Conference. He spoke of the Allegheny Institute as a place of learning for the colored youth of this country; that a complete course of classical education could be obtained there. He said that his hopes were, that in the further progress of his college, young men would be educated for usefulness in the ministry, in schools, and other colleges, etc., and concluded by urging upon the ministers the importance of using their influence among the people, by encouraging them to send their children to schools and to college. He thought the great aims of the Church should be, first, to educate the young men for the ministry, and, second, to educate the entire community for usefulness in society; for our only hope of future elevation under God depended upon this.

To this, Brother D. A. Payne replied, substantially, as follows:

VENERABLE SIR: As one of the Bishops elect in the A. M. E. Church, I have the honor to reply to your appropriate remarks and excellent advice, and in so doing, permit me to say that we highly appreciate all that you have done and said, for we are sensible of the fact that if we are ever elevated to the rights and privileges of American citizens we must become an educated people.

When a mere youth, in my native city, Charleston, S. C., a wealthy planter from the state of North Carolina, who was passing through that city on his way to New Orleans and the West Indies for the improvement of his health, which had been violently attacked by consumption, desired to obtain an intelligent, free young man for his body servant. Application being made to me, through the agency of my guardian, I called at the Planters' Hotel to see him. There he endeavored to persuade me to travel with him, and among the inducements which he plied to my mind was the following statement: Said he, "Daniel, do you know what makes the master and servant? Nothing but superior knowledge—nothing but one man knowing more than another. Now, if you will go with me, the knowledge you may acquire will be of more value to you than three hundred dollars"—the amount of the salary promised by him. Immediately I seized the idea. Instead of going to travel as his servant, I went and chained my mind down to the study of science and philosophy, that I might obtain that knowledge which makes the master.

Sir, in the language of one of England's greatest philosophers, "Knowledge is power;" and the history of nations, as well as that of human progress, fully demonstrates its truthfulness. The most enlightened and powerful nations of the earth were formerly among the most ignorant and powerless; so, also, the most ignorant and imbecile in any given community may, by the same means, become a component part of the most enlightened and powerful in it.

Let every minister, therefore, among us educate himself! Let every mother and father educate their sons and daughters. Then, as water rises to its natural level, so will we rise to the position destined by reason and heaven. This is also the advice of all our real white friends both North and South. As it regards the institution which you have established, my Reverend Sir, we have been there, and have knowledge enough of the students and professors to know that the latter are ripe scholars and Christian gentlemen; that they educate the heads as well as the hearts of their pupils; that they labor to develop all their mental powers, and make them useful members of society. And that this institution is exciting a happy influence on the surrounding communities of Pittsburg and Allegheny is evident to every one who will compare these two communities at the present time with what they were eight years ago.

You, Reverend Sir, are the founder of this institution. The sculptor who takes the rude marble out of the quarry and carves it into a beautiful human figure, immortalizes himself by enshrining his genius in the almost breathing statue, and to him the praise of mankind is due. But what shall be said of or given to that man who takes the rude intellect of human kind, and develops, cultivates and refines it? Sir, he does more to commemorate his name and his greatness than monuments of brass—because he places in heaven such monuments as will live and shine when the blazing stars shall be blotted out from the map of the skies. It now remains for us to do all that is in our power, which is: First, to tender, in the name of our hapless race, our unfeigned thanks for your noble efforts to educate it; and secondly, to do our utmost to promote its prosperity.

GOD

Bishop Daniel A. Payne

Indianapolis
January 1859

REPOSITORY

OF

Religion and Literature.

Vol. II.] INDIANAPOLIS, IND., JANUARY, 1859. [No 1.

RELIGION.

GOD.

BY BISHOP PAYNE.

O thou great and glorious being! What art thou? who can comprehend thee? and who of earth can see thee? A voice from eternity answers, saying, God is love. But what is love? Is it that earthly passion which nestles in human hearts, that to-day is, and to-morrow is not? That sickly sentiment which fills the bosoms of novel writers and novel readers? Or that sweet mysterious feeling which makes a woman leave her mother and her father, and cleave unto her husband? Surely not. This would be reducing thee to a thing, a mere sentiment. 'Tis substituting the fire fly for the blazing sun—a drop of water for the boundless ocean. A man may feel the wind but he cannot tell whence it cometh, nor whither it goeth. So also the christian feels thee. O, divine love! The christian feels thee in his rejoicing heart, and yet he can not tell what is this love, only by echoing the voice from eternity—God is love! And who can comprehend thee? Can mortal man? When this earth can swallow up the universe, then shall finite man be able to comprehend the infinite God. Canst thou by searching find out God? Canst thou find out the Almighty unto perfection? He is higher than heaven—what canst thou do? Deeper than hell—what canst thou know?

Nevertheless, God has condescended to so adapt the intellect of man to the universe, and the universe to his intellect, that by the proper use of the former, and the contemplation of the latter, he may know as much of the Almighty as it is possible to know. The architect is known by his designs, and the skill with which he executes them; the spirit of inspiration saith, even a child is known by his doings, and hence it is also written, that the heavens declare the glory of God, and the firmament showeth his handi-work. And again the invisible things of him from the creation of the world, are clearly seen, being understood by the things that are made, even his eter-nal power and God-head.

My sweet sister, do you see that little flower which grows by the way-side? Pluck it now, place it beneath this pocket microscope. See its expanding petals. That small aperture through which the internal organs were penetrating as fine as the points of cambric needles, are now magnified to the thickness of the gold ring that adorns your delicate finger. Look at the numerous little insects running to and fro, in all the delight of a conscious existence. Their drink is the dew-drop—their food the nectar. There they live, doing the will of their Creator; there they die as soon as that will is accomplished. To them, that little flower is what the globe is to men, their stage of action, their world of probation.

Say, my sister, do you not discern in that flower, the power, wisdom, and goodness of God? And know you not there are more than ten thousand times such flowers as this, which, at the same time that they beautify the hills and valleys of the green earth, also constitute the abodes of myriads of living creatures?

And thou, my dear brother, come, take this telescope, look through the lens to yonder sky, where glitter the countless stars. Each of them is a sun, round which are revolving innumerable planets. Mark the regularity of their motions—their magnitude—their velocity; compared with which, the flight of a swallow is like the motion of a snail.

A thousand times larger than the earth, their revolutions are made with the gracefulness and ease of a humming bird. Boundless as are these orbs, still more innumerable are the living creatures that inhabit them, and endowed with powers which render them able to know, love, and serve the God who made them. Each sun, each planet, each living being, was called into existence by his simple fiat. For he spake, and it was done. He commanded and they were created. Now, when with an angel's sight, you have taken an angel's flight to the most distant star of the most distant constellation glittering upon the azure face of night you have just entered upon the threshhold of a universe whose height is a fathomless depth, and whose depth an immeasurable height, whose length and whose breadth is teeming with an abyss of worlds! See you not, my brother, oh! see you not in all this the wisdom and the power of our God! And are you not prepared to join with Barbould, and say,

With radiant finger contemplation points
To yon blue concave swelled by breath divine
Where one by one, the living eyes of heaven
Awake quick kindling o'er the face of ether,
One boundless blaze, ten thousand trembling fires,
And dancing lusters where the unsteady eye
Restless and dazzled, wanders unconfined,
O'er all this field of glories ; spacious field
And worthy of the Master! he whose hand
With hieroglyphics older than the Nile
Inscribed the mystic tablet hung on high
To public gaze, and said, adore O man,
The finger of thy God. From what pure wells
Of milky light, what soft o'erflowing urn,
Are all these lamps, so filled these friendly
    lamps,
Forever streaming o'er the azure deep,
To point our path and light us to our home.
How soft they slide along their luoid spheres ;
And silent as the foot of time, fulfil
Their destined courses. Nature's self is hushed,
And but a scattered leaf which rustles through
The thick foliage. Not a sound is heard
To break the midnight air, tho' the raised ear,
Intensely listening drinks in every breath.
How deep the silence, yet how loved the praise ;
But are they silent—all ? or is there not
A tongue in every star that talks with man,
And woos him to be wise ? nor woos in vain ;
This dead of midnight is the noon of thought—
And wisdom mounts her zenith with the stars
At this still hour—the self collected soul
Turns inward, and beholds a stranger there
Of high descent, and more than mortal rank
An embryo God ; a spark of fire divine,
Which must burn on for ages when the sun
(Fair transitory creature of a day !)
Has closed his golden eyes, and wrapt in shades,
Forget his wonted journey through the east.

We maintain the position that in a universe whose proportions are as just as they are stupendous; whose forms are as beautiful as they are varied; whose parts and whose movements harmonize with mathematical precision—there is the utterance of an infallible voice, declaring that God is infinite in wisdom, omnipotent in power, and unbounded in goodness. And yet there is another and still higher manifestation which God has given of himself. It is found in the code of moral laws, enacted for the government of moral agents, the fundamental principle of which is this: Thou shalt love the Lord thy God with all thy heart, and thy neighbor as thyself. It is as ample as it is just, and as holy as it is ample, securing all the ends of the most perfect government, both as regards the majesty of the legislator and the happiness of his subjects.

Gabriel, at the right hand of the Eternal, and the meanest slave of Virginia, are placed alike under its glorious and fearful sanctions. So the physical forms of the universe demonstrate the natural attributes of the Most High, so do the moral laws demonstrate the moral perfections of his being.

The trembling that seizes the soul of a man when he is in the act of sinning, and the horrible remorse which follows, reveal the tremendous power of these laws over moral agents. While the deep sweet peace and bounding joy that rushes into the heart when obedience is given to their dictates, demonstrate their adaptedness to secure the happiness of every intelligent and sentient creature.

The heart of the legislator is always seen in the laws he enacts; if he be just, his laws will be just and equitable; if he be a tyrant, his laws will be unjust and tyrannical. So, also, the just and holy laws we have just been contemplating, demonstrate the haracter of the heart of that God whom we love and obey.

But can mortal man behold him? The eagle veils his eyes before he can gaze upon the unclouded sun. Who then can gaze upon the visage of that God whose shadow illumines the sun, and who covers himself with light, as with a garment? Nevertheless the pure in heart shall see God. They shall see him in all his works of nature, providence, and grace. They see him alike in the minute insect, and the huge elephant; in the sagacious mocking bird and the stupid ostrich. They see him sprinkling the earth with flowers, and gilding the firmament with stars! They see him walking with Shadrack, Meshack, and Abednego, in the fiery furnace, and sitting with Daniel in the lion's den. They see him while a babe in the manger, and a man quelling the raging sea amid the howling storm! They see him amid the lightnings and thunders of Sinia, and amid the tears, the groans, and blood of calvary!

ORGANIZATION ESSENTIAL
TO
SUCCESS FOR QUARTO-CENTENNIAL
OF
AFRICAN METHODISM IN THE SOUTH

Bishop Daniel A. Payne

Philadelphia 1890

ORGANIZATION ESSENTIAL TO SUCCESS.

BISHOP DANIEL A. PAYNE, D. D., LL. D.—READ BY REV. I. S. LEE, B. D.

For Quarto-Centennial of African Methodism in the South.

The word Organization is generic and therefore may be applied to any body of men, or women, associated under a written constitution for the accomplishment of some one or more specific purpose; therefore any number of persons, who have agreed to co-operate for scientific pursuits, for the enlargement of the domains of human knowledge, may be called a Scientific Organization; if for philosophical pursuits to enlarge the empire of philosophy, it may be called a Philosophical Organization; or, if to promote the interests of merchants, it may be called a Commercial Organization; but any number of men or women associated for religious purposes, may be called a *Religious Organization*. It may be such an association as the *American Bible Society*, or the *Church Missionary Society*. But whenever a number of men and woman associate for the public worship of the living God, in the house of God, which is the Church of the living God, the ground and pillar of the truth, it may be called an Ecclesiastical Organization, proven to every body and recognized by the common people as the Church. -

But few, very few are they, who comprehend "the house of God," "the Church of the living God," as St. Paul designates her—for his term embraces every man, woman and child bearing the name of Christ, in every land and of every race, color or clime. The majority of people, who are religious, confine the application to their own denomination; others still more narrow-minded, confine its application to a dedicated house, in which they meet to hear preaching, to sing, to pray and to get happy. The Church of the living God is his property which no one man can claim as he has the right to claim his own house, which he has built to shelter himself and his family, or his household. In his letter to the Ephesian christians St. Paul regards the church as the bride of Christ, Eph. v. 22-27. So also St. John "sees her coming down from God out of heaven, prepared as a bride, adorned for her husband." The Elohim, Jehovah, Adonai is her sole lord and master, which he has purchased with the precious and purifying blood of His Beloved Son.

Originally "one unite," the pride, ambition and strife of men have split her outward form into many *divisions* which human device has called denominations. Therefore we have the Presbyterian Church, the Roman Catholic Church, the Lutheran Church, the Church of England, the British Wesleyan Methodist Church, the

Methodist Episcopal Church, the Protestant Episcopal Church, the Baptist Church, the Unitarian and the Quakers, known also as the Society of the Friends. All these are of purely European origin, organized by our white christian brethren and controlled entirely by them. Every one of these were small and insignificant in their beginnings, but Jehovah has enabled every one of them, excepting the Quakers, to develope themselves into numerous and powerful religious bodies, powerful on account of their learning, wealth, influence and resultant usefulness.

Many, if not all of these denominal organizations are the offsprings of internal troubles, quarrels and schisms. In like manner the African Methodist Episcopal Church was born into this world.

    a. Her first appearance was in Philadelphia in 1816.

    b. Her second appearance was in Charleston, S. C., in 1817-18.

    c. In Philadelphia the movement was led by Richard Allen and Daniel Coker, of Baltimore, Md.

    d. In Charleston the movement was led by Morris Brown and Henry Drayton, of Charleston, S. C. This organization embraced about one thousand persons (1817). In 1822 it numbered about three thousand. The leaders of these three thousand were Morris Brown, Henry Drayton, Charles Carr, Amos Cunckshanks, Marcus Brown, Smart Simpson, Harry Bull, John B. Matthews, James Eden, London Turpin, and Aleck Houlston. This band, or little church, was well organized, and had acquired a building lot upon which a commodious but plain house of worship was built. They also owned their own burial ground, or field of graves. Happy among themselves, they were at peace and concord with one another up to 1822. When the contemplated insurrection led by Denmark Vesy, a slave man, was discovered, in destroying which, the civil authorities of the city and state deemed it wise to crush the little band of christians. None of these religious leaders were implicated in the contemplated insurrection. But the love of freedom and the right to worship God according to one's own conscience led Henry Drayton, Charles Carr, father of the gifted and devout Joseph M. Carr; Marcus Brown, and Amos Cunckshanks to follow Morris Brown to Philadelphia. James Eden with a majority of the most intelligent united themselves with the Scotch Presbyterian Church, which was at that time located at the corner of Meeting and Tradd streets, next to the then princely mansion of Nathaniel Russell, esq., the father-in-law of Bishop Theodore Dehone. James Eden, perhaps the most intelligent of those who became members of the Scotch Presbyterian Church, subsequently sailed with the first emmigrants from Charleston to Liberia, where he lived many years, and died respected and lamented by all who knew him. Thus was the African M. E. Church in South Carolina blotted from the pages of Ecclesiastical History. But after the lapse of sixty-eight

years we are here assembled to celebrate the Quarto-Centenary of her
Renaiscence in South Carolina, and of the expansion into Georgia,
Florida, Alabama and Tennessee.

When, how and by whom has her present condition been brought
into existence?   In the spring of 1863 the Rev. C. C. Leigh, a white
preacher of the Methodist Episcopal Church visited the Baltimore
Annual Conference then in session in Baltimore, Md., and desired to
know whether I could send two missionaries to take charge of the
social, moral and religious interests of the Freedmen in South Carolina,
who were like sheep without a shepherd.   I told him I believed I
could.   Then said I to him, "how soon do you want them?"   He said,
"within ten days."   In about ten days Rev. James Lynch, born in
the city of Baltimore and a member of the Baltimore Conference, also
Rev. James D. S. Hall of the New York Conference (then stationed
in Sullivan street A. M. E. Church) were sent into these regions.
They landed at Port Royal and immediately commenced operations
on that island and at Beaufort, afterwards at Charleston, and after that
James Lynch organized a little band at Savannah, Ga.

The two James were very unlike each other.   James Lynch was
always hopeful, James Hall was alw   fearful of coming evil; Lynch
was the bold lion, Hall the timid sheep; Hall was the witty Irishman,
Lynch the sagacious statesman; Lynch was born to be the skillful or-
ganizer, Hall the trembling follower, ready to run away from the ranks
at the barking of a rat-tarrier, or the howling of a bull-dog.   Each of
these missionaries worked successfully, according to their heaven be-
stowed ability, and made it possible for the organization of the South
Carolina Conference on Monday morning, May 16, 1865.   That took
place in the Colored Presbyterian Church, Calhoun street.   The two
itinerant elders were James Lynch and James A. Handy; the two
licentiates were James H. A. Johnson and Theophilus G. Stewart—
these licentiates from the North were subsequently ordained deacons.
A local preacher named William Bently constituted the five persons
present at the opening of the South Carolina Conference.   Subsequently
Elder R. H. Cain from the New York Conference, Elder Anthony L.
Stanford and George A. Rue from the New England Conference were
added.   The natives of the state who joined the South Carolina Conference were Charles L. Bradwell, N. Murphy, Robert Taylor and
Richard Vanderhorse.   The whole number of persons within the
boundaries of the South Carolina Conference was supposed to be about
4000.   That number embraced North Carolina, South Carolina and
Georgia, along the coasts and all the islands.   Reports on temperance,
education and missions were discussed and adopted; an Historic and
Literary Society was formed, also a Preachers' Aid Society.   Thus
equipped the South Carolina Conference, like an armed ship launched,
was sent forth to conquer the lands of the South.

The greater number of these 4000 people had been members of the M. E. Church South, others had been converted through the ministry of Lynch and Hall. Here was a field broad, long and rich in its soil. But can any field take care of itself? No. Left to itself briers, brambles and weeds will soon over run it. To develope its possibilities there is need of stout, intelligent laborers, system and order; also an overseer skilled in farming, to direct the movements of the laborers, to work out the system and to preserve the order of the whole, as regards time, place and manner. All these things are *essential* for successful farming, and this is organization. Here was also a multitude of men and women who called themselves Soldiers of the Cross. But there was no one sufficiently trained to classify and arrange them into an effective army. Therefore they needed an officer trained in the military school, who had experience in the battle field, to classify and arrange them into companies and regiments, then to put them under the drill of good Captains and Colonels, Brigadier-Generals and Major-Generals, these all under one Commander-in-Chief to control their movements in time of peace, and especially in time of war. But from the Commander-in-Chief down to the Corporal law and order must be respected voluntarily by all, if not compulsion must be used to maintain government. This is another illustration of organization. But the divine idea of organization is given by St Paul in the 2d epistle to the Corinthian Church, xii, 4-27, which is taken from the splendid structure of the human body, in which we see the arms completed by the hands, and the legs by the feet; two eyes are set in the face to see how to operate the hands and the feet; there are two ears also to listen to the sounds which strike the tympanum, while the eyes look around to see whence, from whom and from what the sounds proceed. Then are all the parts dependent upon one another as related and necessary to the beauty and efficient operation of the entire person. But of what value are all these related members if there were no intellect to direct and control their movements and operations, and no power to say, "I will or will not, you shall or you shall not?"

Now we see that the Apostle used this figure to indicate the ecclesiastical organization of his day, and to prove that organization of the whole church of the living God was essential to its existence, its expansion and its perpetuity. His metaphor also teaches us that while organization is essential to success, there are certain elements in which it must involve in order that it might be a living and perpetual force, generating life as the breath in the human being, and diffusing life through all its parts, purging itself of all that is injurious to its nature. What are these essential elements to the organism, essential to its vigorous perpetuity. Harmony must be in it; involve at its birth if possible, if not before its birth. Harmony signifies concord or agreement in facts, opinions, manners or interests. So says Webster. Crabb

D

says it means aptitude of minds to coalesce.   It is mostly employed
for those who are in close connection and obliged to co-operate.   Conflict is the opposite to harmony.   Therefore if conflict obtains for any
length of time it will develope into antagonism and endanger the existence of the organization.   If antagonism becomes fixed in its heart,
disintegration will be the result.   Harmony in regard to facts, opinions,
sentiments and interests will bind the members together, and be ever
invigorating and stimulating all to labor as one man for the attainment
of the same end.

And another element of life in an organization is unity of motion,
unity in planning and unity in executing the measures which have
been approved and adopted.   Unity regarding the character of the
agents who are to be chosen from the candidates for official positions
in the organism.   If this kind of unity can be obtained, the organization will be preserved, strengthened, enlarged and perpetuated from
ages to ages.   The chief apostle doubtless had this principle in contemplation when he commanded and urged the church at Ephesus to
endeavor to keep the unity of the spirit in the bonds of peace.   Unity
of the spirit is unity of judgment, affection and feeling among those
who constitute the body of Christ.   So says Dr. Scarff.   On this subject Dr Clarke says: "By the unity of the spirit means to understand, not only a spiritual unity, but also a unity of sentiments, desires and affections, such as one worthy, and springs from the spirit of
God,"—what the infallible head of the church inspired St. Paul to
write the church at Ephesus.   He promisee by the pen of Jeremiah
to bestow upon the Jewish church—Jeremiah xxxii, ——which element he emphasized in his sacerdotal prayer beseeching the Father that
the whole church "may be one," as he is in the Father, and the
Father in Him.   That they all may be perfect in one, John xvii, 21,
That all may be one.   This oneness produces perfection through all
nature.   It produces both beauty and goodness in the church of the
living God, every branch of it, in every twig of every branch.

We now call your attention to some evils which can break up an
ecclesiastical organization, among every and any age.

The revaulting ambition of a bold, restless man, whose tongue *is
full of fire*, as ignorant people call it, but which educated and intelligent persons justly denounce as "flippant oratory and glittering
rhetoric."   The revaulting ambition of Absolum raised a revolt against
the throne of his own father, and would have overthrown it if God had
not pledged and used omnipotence to perpetuate it.   Thus like Absolum
the ambitious will employ deception, suppression and the lowest means,
even murder, to obtain the *goal*, be it crown or *Bishopric*.   It therefore
becomes the duty of upright men to guard the ecclesiastical organization against the ambitious leaders of the people.   So also envy may

disturb the peace, break the harmony and disintegrate the ecclesiastical organization.

Relationships as well as pretended friendships are sometimes employed by envy to produce discord, antagonism and destruction to an ecclesastical organization. It was this infernal spirit that moved Aaron the brother and Miriam the sister of Moses against that chosen and faithful leader of Israel, and they doubtless would have succeeded in disorganizing the encampment if God himself had not defended his servant, Moses, and smitten Miriam with leprosy. See Numbers xii, 1-15. So also the envy Korah Dathan and Abiram would have disintegrated the church in the wilderness if Jehovah had not made the quaking earth open her mouth and swallow them up. But how great was the suffering of that consecrated hoast? The result of these three envious rivals of Moses was the death of 14,240 persons. Therefore every ecclesiastical organizatton ought to guard itself against the envious church leader.

Ungodliness within the ecclesiastical organization can destroy it. This evil utterly destroyed the Jewish Church, and swept from the face of the earth the seven churches of Asia. Notwithstanding all these evils to which organization is exposed, it is essential to the success of both state and church. Because organization is government. Destroy that and the state falls into anarchy. Destroy that and the church disintegrates. Without organization the birth of any denomination is impossible. Witfield went through this country publishing salvation in all places, but organizing no churches, and therefore his converts have no existence at the present hour. Wesley organized one in the city of New York, and that one has multiplied itself into tens of thousands, into millions, and thus the Conference organized at Charleston May 16, 1865, has produced eleven vigorous conferences, and the four thousand souls have multiplied themselves into more than a hundred thousand. To Him that sitteth upon the throne, and to the lamb that was slain be all the glory, all the honor, all the wisdom, all the riches, all the praise forever and ever, amen.

THE RELATIONS OF THIS CONFERENCE
WITH
THE AFRICAN METHODIST CHURCH

Bishop Daniel A. Payne

Boston 1868

The next topic in order was:

THE RELATIONS OF THIS CONFERENCE WITH THE AFRICAN METHODIST CHURCH,

which, after a few explanatory remarks by Rev. Charles Lowe, was introduced by Bishop Payne, of Wilberforce University, Xenia, Ohio, as follows:

It is proper that I should say a few words that may not seem just to the point, before I address myself to the subject before us. I wish to say, that, in forming a connection with the American Unitarian Association, the African Methodist Episcopal Church do not desire what is popularly called affiliation, because we believe affiliation would fetter our moral liberty, prevent freedom of thought, fetter our expression of what we believe to be true. Neither do we desire union with your talented, learned and venerable Association, because this would be absorption, ecclesiastically. Neither do we desire isolation from our Christian brethren in these United States, because that would be stagnation and death. It would be throwing us back into Africa, back into India, back to the heathen ideas of God and humanity. But we desire co-operation with your venerable body; we desire mutual attraction, if I may use that term; you attracting us by your generous spirit, we attracting you by our absolute necessities and wants. And this is the law of attraction.

We are willing to co-operate with you, we believe in the generosity of your religious principles, we believe in the godlike nature of the spirit which you manifest, — perfectly unselfish, and having no desire beyond that of blessing sinful humanity. You can do us good in this co-operation and we can do you good. If you have seed to be sown, we have the soil, the rich, the luxurious, the fertile soil, in which you can sow that seed,— the seed of immortal, heaven-born truth. We have the soil for that which will bring forth, in due season, the rich fruits of righteousness and good works, to the glory of God and the wellbeing of our common humanity.

Then again if you have the strength to impart power to us, we are ready to receive that power. If you have wisdom to assist us in entering upon a line of usefulness on which we have never entered before, — I mean the great work of Christian education among the people of the South; I mean the great work of training immortal minds to be educators of other minds,—we can co-operate with you in that work. We have a noble band of young men and women at our school; young men and women highly gifted by nature, and I will say, yet more richly endowed with the spirit of Christ. They have intellect, they are getting learning, and they have already been put in possession by God of that wonderful power which subdues the will of man and subjugates the affections of the soul to the power of divine truth. They have consecrated themselves to Christ; they have laid themselves upon the altar of Christian usefulness, there to smoke and to burn until life itself becomes extinct. They have given themselves to Christ, to God, and to humanity. We want you to help us in cultivating these minds, in sanctifying these hearts, in securing these immortal powers to the service of that great Redeemer who came down from heaven to suffer and die that we might live for ever. That we may do this, we ask you to give us money. We can never hope to give it back, but be sure, Mr. President, it will be "recompensed at the resurrection of the just."

The subject was further discussed by Mr. Tanner, Editor of an African Methodist newspaper, and Bishop Brown, of the African Methodist Church.

Miss Amy Bradley made an appeal in behalf of her Mission Schools for poor whites in North Carolina.

On motion of Rev. C. A. Staples, a collection was taken up in furtherance of Miss Bradley's mission, amounting to $645.

Adjourned to Friday morning.

SEMI-CENTENNIAL SERMON

Bishop Daniel A. Payne

Cincinnati 1874

SEMI-CENTENNIAL SERMON.

AFTERNOON SERVICES, COMMENCING AT 2½ O'CLOCK.

The auditorium and balconies were filled to their utmost capacity. Bishop Payne gave out the hymn commencing—

> " Jesus, the name high over all,
>   In hell, or earth, or sky."

The choir sang it with good effect; after which the Bishop addressed the Throne of Grace fervently and eloquently.

The choir then sang the chant—

> " Holy now is this place."

Rev. Robert A. Johnson, of Columbus, O., then read the second chapter of 2nd Timothy.

Bishop Daniel A. Payne, D. D., presiding officer of the Third
Episcopal District, and president of Wilberforce University, delivered the following discourse:

**THE DIVINELY APPROVED WORKMAN, OR THE MINISTRY FOR ALLEN
TEMPLE DURING THE NEXT FIFTY YEARS.**

"Study to show thyself approved unto God, a workman that need-
eth nor to be ashamed, rightly dividing the word of truth.
"And the servant of the Lord must not strive; but be gentle unto
all men, apt to teach, patient,
"In meekness instructing those that oppose themselves; if God
peradventure will give them repentence, to the acknowledging of
the truth."—2 TIMOTHY ii. 15, 24, 25.

The word workman implies work to be done, and a master to
oversee the work that is to be done.   It also implies a house, an
edifice, a temple; more or less important, more or less grand,
more or less durable; lasting for centuries, accommodating generation after generation.   This supposition covers the facts of
the case to be considered; because the Church of God is called
" the house of God," "a Holy Temple," " the Temple of the
Living God."   But this temple is a spiritual temple; the workman, therefore, must do spiritual work in this spiritual temple;
and his work is all the while under the sleepless eye of the Omniscient Master, who is solicitious about the manner as well as
the ability of the workman, because this temple is of the highest importance, as well as of vast dimensions, and of durability
embracing all time and all the races, therefore, all the generation
of men.   Now each local church is nothing more, nothing less,

than a chamber in this Spiritual Temple, concerning the purity, the finish, and beauty of which the Divine Master is equally interested. Let the workman, therefore, acquit himself accordingly. But to do this the workman should study the character of his master, as well as the work which is to be done. And this leads us to the first thing in the text which is to be expounded; that is the question. What is to be studied? First, he must study God, in order that he may learn the character of the master whom he has to serve, and conform his own character to that master's will. Now God has manifested and is manifesting himself, in three different ways. The workman, therefore, will do well to study these threefold manifestations of the Deity.

a. The first is Nature around us. We cannot open our eyes or ears without seeing forms and hearing voices, speaking in behalf of an existing but invisible Deity. In these we shall find proofs of his wisdom, power, and goodness, and recognize the fact that these attributes are infinite.

b. In history we also have manifestations of God. In the origin, progress, complete development of a nation's greatness-with its decline, old age, and death, in which we see exhibitions of the retributive justice and providence of God as the Almighty Ruler of races and nations, of kingdoms and empires; humbling the arrogant pride of despots, as in the case of Nebuchadnezzar; exalting the humble and the wise, as in the case of Daniel; punishing crime, as in the case of David, and rewarding incorruptable virtue, as in the person of Joseph; breaking the arm of the brazen-hearted and blasphemous enslaver, as he did that of Pharaoh; and out of an enslaved race to produce a great people, as is illustrated by the history of the Israelites. Nor does God manifest himself in the history of races, nations, and governments only; he does this also in that kind of personal history which we call Biography. No one, that is, no thinking mind, can read the biograpy of Joseph or Job, of Abraham or Jacob among the Patriarchs, or of Luther and Wesley among the Reformers, without discovering an invisible, supernatural power behind and above these men, inspiring, guiding, protecting them, planning their plans and executing their victories, attributable to none other than the omniscient Almighty beneficent Being, whom we recognize as God, and whom we are ever wont to call the God of Abraham, Isaac, and Jacob.

c. But above all these there is Revelation, in which the Infinite has manifested himself as he has done no where else. In physical nature we see exhibitions of his infinite wisdom, power, and goodness. In history we have evidences of his inflexible justice and beneficent providence, as well as his unquestionable sovereignty. But in Revelation we see his mercy, moving hand in hand with his justice; his unutterable love hand in hand with his immaculate holiness, and all these directed and controlled by his unerring wisdom, constraining the philosophic mind to exclaim, "O! the depth of the riches, both of the wisdom and knowledge of God! How unsearchable are his judgments, and his ways past finding out."

Now, when the studious workman has prosecuted such studies, and made such researches as we have indicated, he will feel the necessity of unceasing efforts to secure the approbation of God, from whom he professes to have received a commission to preach the Gospel, and consequently of so conducting himself in the presence of his Omniscient Master, that he may never have cause to be ashamed.

d But of what may this workman be ashamed? Of two things: of his ignorance and of his vices. So varied and so deep are the truths with which the Christian minister has to deal, that, unless he is a careful, prayerful, and diligent student of that one book, the Bible, he will often be compelled to blush at his ignorance. And let this workman know that to understand that one, as it ought to be understood, and to apply its varied important teachings as they ought to be applied, it is necessary that he make himself master of many other books.

Revelation! we say, Revelation is the field above all which the Christian workman must study, in order that he may become acquainted with the ineffable character of his Lord and Master; for there he will find out the truth, that so august a Sovereign demands a servant of no mean character. The dignity and benignity of this Master will impress themselves so deeply upon his understanding and his affections, that he will be disposed to conform his own character to that of his Master.

The slaves of educated and opulent masters in South Carolina always felt themselves as having a standing and character better than the slaves of ignorant and poverty stricken masters. So also the embassador of a great and powerful empire feels a dignity and importance, which he who represents a State of small resources and feeble power can not possibly feel. Now what is true of such servants ought to be far more true of the man who represents the *King* of kings, and *Lord* of lords.

e But, there is another source of knowledge concerning the Deity which this workman must also study. *It is man* in his three fold nature. His physical, mental, and moral—his spiritual nature. In the former he will find a manifestation of wisdom, skill, power, and goodness, which at once demonstrates the character of the Master whom he serves.

A study of the mental nature of man will increase the evidence of the almightiness and infinite wisdom of his Master, and an acquaintance with his moral nature will serve to give him still greater evidences of the glorious character of the Infinite. The spiritual nature of his being is the crystalization of his moral, as his moral is the sublimation of his mental. In him you will see a wonderful blending of weakness and strength, of good and evil; the qualities of a devil alternating with those of an angel, with the attributes of a worm blending with those of a god. In him you will find the heart that weeps and bleeds, that hopes and fears, that hates and loves, that crawls in the dust and wings its flight toward heaven. In him you shall see the *will*, that now moves backward with the stubborness of a mule, and then onward with the alacrity of a seraph. So that, in the study of man the Christian workman will find the answer to the question of the inspired poet: "What is man, that thou art mindful of him? and the son of man that thou visitest him?"

O, there is such a length and breadth, such a height and depth, such variety and richness, such beauty and sublimity, such joy in these studies, in these researches, that the intelligent workman, who is anxious to secure the divine approbation, will have no time for mere amusements, gossip, or indolence.

Let this workman so study that he shall not have occasion to be ashamed of his ignorance. But the Christian workman may also be ashamed of a vice contracted in his previous life, which is called the besetting sin. Let the workman beware of this evil against which there is no shield, but the covert of the Savior's wings. There the believer is safe; from the grasp of his omnipotent hand no power can pluck him. But this implies holy living—*not impeachability*, but eternal vigilance against sin, persistent opposition to temptation ; and where resistance itself might result in defeat to find safety in flight, but the asylum to which he flies is none other than the covert of the Almighty wings. To love all men so that we shall always be devising and executing for their well being, including even the man whom we may partly regard as an enemy. Love to all will make us do justice to all; and such a man, who thus loves, will always find himself at one with the Judge of all the Earth, therefore approved by Him. This love is sometimes called godliness, by which is meant the thinking, planning and executing for the well-being of all. Of this manner of life, this kind of moral conduct, a workman shall never have occasion to be ashamed.

f. Moreover, this workman must not strive; or he must not be contentious, quarrelsome, threatening those who oppose him with personal violence, treating as enemies all who differ from him in opinion, in principles or measures. But he must be patiently instructing those who oppose themselves. There are men who cannot see the right, the true, or the good. Men who oppose these things are opposed to themselves; because these are beneficial to all. Meekly teaching the ignorant, because it is right; and meekly teaching the opposers of the truth, in order that God may grant them repentence, and cause them to obey and defend that which they have been so ready to oppose. Such must be the workman who may fill this pulpit in the future. They will be needed to lead the future interests of this church; they will be needed to lead on the future interests of our growing connection.

And now it is time that we should review the history of this local church of the Church Militant, in order that we may see what it has accomplished, and learn what it may and must do for future conquests in behalf of God and man. Besides the development and establishment of itself, from a very small and weak beginning into a numerous and powerful society, it has planted a small and at present a weak congregation on Walnut Hills. Is this work enough for half century? I think not; I think it ought to have accomplished more than this. I feel certain that if its membership had been alive to the work of Christ, more could have been accomplished. Instead of one powerful church, we might have had three or four. " He that soweth sparingly shall reap sparingly." " According to thy faith, so shall it be unto thee." Again, what has this church done for Christian education? Our dear Brother Arnett tells us that of 21 colored teachers, now employed in the colored schools of Cincinnati, nine are members of our two churches, or are attached to them, *i. e.* worship statedly in them. This is a handsome proportion; because, besides ours, there are six other churches. But did Allen Temple educate these nine teachers by direct efforts put forth on her part? Let the officers of Allen Temple answer. Again, did Allen Temple ever send a young man to Wilberforce to prepare himself for the work of the Christian ministry, and having sent one there, did she ever support him until his educational course was completed? If you have enjoyed the ministry of men wholly or partially educated, was it, or was it not, because they were forced upon you by circumstances beyond your control, or rather by your direct agency? Is it not generally true that our progress in an educational direction may be likened to that which the freight trains make along the railroad? But if this has been the case in the past, it ought not to be so in the future. We ought to put forth systematic and direct efforts for our own progress in all that is good and useful. As a denomination, we have done well in planning and building churches, during the last half century; let us now go to work to plan and to build schools of learning. Let this church plan for, and systematically educate her young men for the ministry. Let the official board lead the way by planning the work, and I am certain the people, *i. e.*, the members of this church, will sustain them in their efforts; so, at the end of every five or six years, this church can be sending out a young man well prepared to be a workman approved unto God.

There are also your daughters. These ought to be the objects of your special regard. To educate them in such a manner as to render them fit to do Christian work, is the highest duty of the church to herself. She can perform none higher, none more beneficial for the community. And whenever a young woman of talents and piety is found, who has aptness for teaching, and who is desirous to qualify herself thoroughly for such a work, but has not the means to meet the expenses, this church ought to undertake to educate her. Perhaps there is no greater power in a given community than that of educated women. I use the term in its broadest, highest sense, by which I do not mean a smattering, or even excellence in music, instrumental and vocal, in drawing and painting; nor yet do I mean a mere classical or scientific and mathematical training; but I do mean a Christian education, that which draws out head and heart towards the Cross, while after consecrating them to the Cross, sends the individuals from beneath the Cross with the spirit of Him who died upon it; sends them abroad well fitted for Christian usefulness, a moral, a spiritual power, moulding, coloring community, and preparing it for a nobler and higher state of existence in that world where change never comes, unless it be a change from the good to the better, and from the better to the best.

The past, the dark past, is gone; I hope forever gone. It was the time when ignorance sat in high places and ruled, when vice was as much respected as virtue. The present and the future demands a different spirit and different conduct. The almighty fiat is gone forth. "Many shall run to and fro, and knowledge shall be increased." Hence, the future demands educated women, in order that there may be educated wives, consequently educated mothers, who will give unto the race a training entirely and essentially different from the past. In other words, the future demands wives and mothers who will, like Susanna Wesley, convert the homestead into a school house, and that school house into a church, where the young immortals shall be trained for their heavenward flight. The wants of the race demand such women to descend into the South as educators, to assist in correcting the religious errors of the freedmen, and to bridle their wild enthusiasm. The religious errors, the wild enthusiasm of the freedmen, are results of the slavery which had been operating upon them and their forefathers for nearly two hundred and fifty years, and cannot be removed in a day, nor by one man, nor one kind of human agency. Deity does not operate upon humanity after that fashion. He applies a multitude of instrumentalities and different agencies to civilize and Christianize a race; among which are the educators of a race, but of these none are more potent than the educated wife, the educated mother, the educated school-mistress, but educated under the Cross, and in the spirit of him who died upon the Cross.

There is also the work of Christian Missions at home and abroad. A careful and impartial review of the history of Allen Temple shows that in this direction she has done but little. This sturdy tree, during the past fifty years, should have sent its roots *under* the Ohio, if it could not send them across it; and by this time there should have been at least two young trees vigorously flower. ing and fruiting on the soil of Kentucky. But we have said let the past errors and blunders be buried with the past. At the same time let us study the fact, that a new leaf, with its pages, has been added to the volume of our history; nor let us study this fact alone, let us go beyond that to its philosophy, which lies behind and beneath it. In so doing, we will learn the great lesson which history teaches, that every revolution which passes over a nation *evolves* principles which, while they appear new, are really as old as humanity, and which were involved into its very nature, at its conception in the mind of the Creator; that these principles give birth to new sentiments, new laws, new cus- toms, which the Church of God must consider and take into ac- count in all her subsequent operations; and that the denomination of Christians, or that particular branch of a denomination which will not take these changes into consideration, and act accord- ingly must become extinct. Progressive humanity, led on by the hand of its Omnipotent Father, will leave it behind like a ship on the sand bar, or tread it out as salt that has lost its savor. In either case the extinction of such a denomination, or such a local society of Christians, is as certain as the extinction of the Jewish Church. Christianity is an educating power. It educates in every direction that touches humanity; not religously only, but morally also; not morally only, but intellectually also; not intellectually only, but, because it is a religious, moral, and intel- lectual educational power, it logically affects and modifies all the forms of civil and political life.

Now the important question that Allen Temple has to consider and determine is: will she become an educating and missionary power as Christ Jesus designs her to be? or will she refuse. There are two negative ways in which she may answer this question. The one by a direct and positive *no,* and the other by *pleading poverty.* Either of these answers will prove fatal to her influence, prosperity, and perpetuity. Therefore, the only *wise* answer she can give is: "Lo I come to do thy will, O God!" To be willing to do is to get the power to do. Let Allen Temple resolve to edu- cate and to assist in spreading the Redeemer's kingdom from pole to pole: then let her *immediately execute* this resolution by organized systematic, and persistent efforts, and the means will be supplied by Him who has said, "ask and it shall be given to you; seek and ye shall find!"

Let Allen Temple take this advice, which is calmly and considerately given, and she will make a grand, a glorious history during the next fifty years. To educate the immortal mind and prepare it for eminent usefulness on earth, and the unutterable glory of heaven; to assist in transforming this dark earth into the "Holy City—new Jerusalem," is a work in which the cherubim and seraphim would be happy to labor. O that God would give to Allen Temple the Missionary, the educating, spirit, the mind that was in Jesus Christ.

At the conclusion of the sermon by Bishop Payne. The choir sang the chant "How beautiful is Zion."

Bishop Payne, assisted by Rev. R. A. Johnson, ordained Thomas Elias Knox a local deacon; the services were solemn and interesting, after which Rev. B. W. Arnett baptized the following named children: James Spotswood Fleming Robinson, Ann Maria Turner, Augustus Allen, Estella Scott, Arthur Castella S Phelps, Levenia Anderson, William Edward Shaw, Miree Spencer.

The collection was continued from the morning, and quite a number contributed.

Benediction by Rev. Jermiah Lewis.

WELCOME

TO

THE RANSOMED;

OR,

DUTIES

OF THE

COLORED INHABITANTS

OF THE

DISTRICT OF COLUMBIA.

———•◦•———

BALTIMORE:

PRINTED BY BULL & TUTTLE, CLIPPER OFFICE.

1862.

GEORGETOWN, **D. C.**, April 14, 1862.

REVEREND BISHOP PAYNE,

Dear Sir—We, the undersigned, having listened carefully to your Sermon, preached at the A. M. E. Ebenezer Church, on Sabbath last, April 13th, a day set apart by the Colored Churches in Georgetown and Washington as a day of Thanksgiving and Prayer, in view of Emancipation in the District, and being deeply impressed by its appropriateness, its wisdom, and valuable practical advice; and believing that such a sermon should be within the reach of all the colored people of this District and the United States; we therefore solicit you to allow us to print the same in pamphlet form.

> JAMES LYNCH, *Preacher in Charge.*
> PLATO LEE,
> JOHN F. LEE,
> H. BATSON,
> CLEMENT BECKETT,
> WILSON HAWKINS.

WASHINGTON, D. C., April 18, 1862.

DEAR BRETHREN:

Yours of the 14th instant has been received. In compliance with the request which it contains, I send you herewith a copy of the discourse preached last Sunday in the Ebenezer Chapel, Georgetown, D. C. It is identically the same in all its parts. I have amplified some of its thoughts, and added three or four notes, which I think valuable and useful.

That its teachings may be productive of good to those for whom it was prepared, and bring glory to Him, who is High over all and blessed for ever, is the fervent prayer of

> Your humble servant,
> DANIEL A. PAYNE.

To REV. JAMES LYNCH *and others.*

WELCOME TO THE RANSOMED;

—OR,—

Duties of the Colored Inhabitants of the District of Columbia.

I. TIM. 2, 1—4.

St. Paul addressed the Epistles to Timothy, the young Bishop of Ephesus, for the purpose of giving him instructions touching the false doctrines inculcated by certain false teachers, as well as instructions respecting the qualifications of the Christian ministry, their duties to themselves, to God, and the flock committed by the Holy Spirit to their special guidance.

But foremost of all the duties which he enjoined upon the Ephesian ministry and laity were those of making "Supplications, prayers, intercessions, and giving of thanks for all men." For men in general, embracing the whole family of Adam, in all their *varieties* as nations, tribes, communities, peoples.

This is God-like, because the Eternal loves all, and manifests the infinity of his nature, by his universal care for all mankind. In this, He also demonstrates His universal Fatherhood, and thereby establishes the brotherhood of man.

But guided by the benevolence of unerring wisdom, the Apostle descends from a general to a particular statement of the case, and *commands* us to single out from among the nations of the earth their chieftains—*Kings* and *authorities*—for whom we are to make special "Supplications, prayers, intercessions, and giving of thanks."

To the cheerful and fervent performance of this gracious work, he presses several [motives upon us—"that we may live

a quiet and peaceable life in all godliness and honesty''—
because "it is good and acceptable in the sight of God our
Saviour"—because God "will have all men to be saved and to
come unto the knowledge of the truth." Let us briefly trace
out this line of thought.

To supplicate, is to *implore* God *submissively*. To pray to
God, is to adore Him for His glorious perfection, to confess our
sins to Him, and to beseech Him for mercy and pardon. To
intercede with God is to entreat Him by the fervent, effectual
prayer of faith, to be reconciled to offending man. This we
may do as well for our enemies as for our friends.

We are gathered to celebrate the emancipation, yea, rather,
the *Redemption* of the enslaved people of the District of Columbia, the exact number of whom we have no means of ascer-
taining, because, since the benevolent intention of Congress
became manifest, many have been removed by their owners
beyond the reach of this beneficent act.

Our pleasing task then, is to welcome to the Churches, the
homesteads, and circles of free colored Americans, those who
remain to enjoy *the boon of holy Freedom*.

Brethren, sisters, friends, we say welcome to our Churches,
welcome to our homesteads, welcome to our social circles.

Enter the great family of Holy Freedom; not to *lounge in
sinful indolence*, not to *degrade yourselves by vice*, nor to *corrupt
society by licentiousness*, neither to *offend the laws by crime*, but
to the *enjoyment of a well regulated liberty*, the offspring of
generous laws; of law as just as generous, as righteous as just—
a liberty to be *perpetuated* by equitable law, and sanctioned by
the divine; for law is never equitable, righteous, just, until it
harmonizes with the will of Him, who is "*King* of kings, and
Lord of lords," and who commanded Israel to *have but one law
for the home-born* and the *stranger*.

We repeat ourselves, welcome then *ye ransomed ones;* welcome *not* to indolence, to vice, licentiousness, and crime, but to
a well-regulated liberty, sanctioned by the Divine, maintained
by the Human law.

Welcome to habits of industry and thrift—to duties of religion and piety—to obligations of law, order, government—of
government divine, of government human: these two, though

not one, are inseparable. The man who refuses to obey divine law, will never obey human laws. *The divine first*, the *human next*. The latter is the consequence of the former, and follows it as light does the rising sun.

We invite you to our Churches, because we desire you to be religous; to be more than religious; we urge you *to be godly*. We entreat you to never be content until you are emancipated from sin, from sin without, and from sin within you. But this kind of freedom is attained only through the faith of Jesus, love for Jesus, obedience to Jesus. As certain as the American Congress has *ransomed* you, so certain, yea, more certainly has Jesus redeemed you from the guilt and power of sin by his own precious blood.

As you are now free in body, so now seek to be free in soul and spirit, from sin and Satan. The *noblest freeman is he whom Christ makes free*.

We invite you to our homesteads, in order that we may aid you as well by the power of good examples as by the beauty of holy precept, in raising up intelligent, virtuous, pious, happy families. We invite you to our social circles, in order that you may have none of those inducements which grow out of a mere love of society, to frequent the *gambling hells*, and groggeries, which gradually lead their votaries to infamy and the pit that is bottomless.

Permit us, also, to advise you to seek every opportunity for the cultivation of your minds. To the adults we say, enter the Sunday Schools and the Night Schools, so opportunely opened by Dr. Pierson, in behalf of the American Tract Society. In these latter you can very soon learn to read the precious word of God, even before you shall have a familiar knowledge of the letters which constitute the alphabet.

Rest not till you have learned to read the Bible. 'Tis the greatest, the best of books. In it is contained the Divine law. O! meditate therein by day and by night, for "the law of the Lord is perfect, converting the soul; the testimony of the Lord is sure, making wise the simple; the statutes of the Lord are right, rejoicing the heart; the commandment of the Lord is pure, enlightening the eyes;—more to be desired are they than gold, yea, than much fine gold; sweeter also than honey and

the honeycomb." *"In keeping of them there is great reward."*
Yield uniform, implicit obedience to their teachings. They
will purify your hearts and make them the abodes of the Ever-
Blessed Trinity.

When you shall have reached this point, you will be morally
prepared to recognize and respond to all the relations of civilized and christianized life.

But of the children take *special care.* Heaven has entrusted
them to you for a *special purpose.* What is that purpose? Not
merely to eat and to drink, still less to *gormandize.* Not
merely to dress finely in broadcloths, silks, satins, jewelry, nor
to dance to the sound of the tamborine and fiddle; but *to learn
them how to live and how to die—to train them for great usefulness on earth—to prepare them for greater glory in heaven.*

Keep your children in the schools, even if you have to eat
less, drink less and wear coarser raiments; though you eat but
two meals a day, purchase but one change of garment during
the year, and relinquish all the luxuries of which we are so
fond, but which are as injurious to health and long life as they
are pleasing to the taste.

Let the education of your children penetrate the heart.—
That education which forgets, or purposely omits, the culture
of the heart, *is better adapted to devilism than manhood.* But
the education which reaches the heart, moulds it, humbles it
before the Cross, is rather the work of the homestead than the
common school or the college. It is given by the *parents*
rather than the schoolmaster—by the *mother* rather than the
father.

How important, then, that the mothers be *right-minded;* that
our young women, of whom our mothers come, be brought up
with a high sense of personal character—be taught to prefer
virtue to gold, and death itself rather than a violated chastity.
The women make the men; therefore the women should be
greater than the men, in order that they be the mothers of
great men. I mean good men, *for none are great who are not
good.*

But this requires the transforming grace of God; requires
that our mothers be women of strong faith and fervent daily
prayers; requires that they live beneath the wings of the Cheru-

bim—at the foot of the Cross—loving the God-man "whose favor is life, and whose loving kindness is better than life."

Such mothers will care for the heart education of their children, and will consequently lay continuous siege to the Throne of God in behalf of their sons and daughters, even as the Syrophœnician mother importuned the compassionate Jesus in behalf of her afflicted daughter, or as Queen Esther did Ahasuerus in behalf of her menaced kinsmen.

Such mothers will carefully train their children, as Moses was trained by his mother, preserving him pure from *the vices of a Court* and the baneful examples of lordly superiors; or, like Susanna Wesley, will educate their sons, as she did John and Charles, in the atmosphere of such spiritual excellence, and with such a moral power, as will make them ministering angels of good to man and glory to God Most High.

Lastly—Let us advise you respecting money. Some people value it too much, others too little. Of these extremes take the medium; for money has its proper value. That value *lies in its adaptedness to promote the ends of Christian enlightenment;* to purchase the best medical aid and other comforts in the days of affliction; to administer to the wants of old age, and to enable us to assist in making mankind wiser and better.

But how are we to get money? Get it by diligent labor. Work, work, work! Shun no work that will bring you an honest penny. 'Tis honorable to labor with our own hands. God works, and shall man be greater than God? Fools only think labor dishonorable. Wise men feel themselves honored in following the example of God, whose works adorn and bless both heaven and earth.

But when you get the pennies save them. Then you will soon have dollars. The dollars will enable you to buy comfortable homes for yourselves and your children.

You can save your pennies—yea, dollars—if you will *run away* from whiskey, rum and tobacco. A few years ago an intelligent minister said that the colored people of the District of Columbia spent ten thousand dollars a year for tobacco.— What a sum for poison! Better take that money to build churches and school houses; better take it to obtain and pay

2

thoroughly educated teachers for your pulpits and your school houses—*the schoolmasters* as well as the preachers.

Work for money; work every day, work diligently, and *save your money when you get it*.

Be *obliging* and *faithful* to your employers, and you will be sure to keep your places. Never be above your business.— Many a man has ruined himself and his family by this foolish pride.

Ever since the first stone in the foundations of the Universe was laid by God's own hand till now, he has been working, and will continue working through endless ages. Follow his glorious example. Work, work, work, for an honest penny; but when you get it, pause and think three times before you spend it; but when you spend it, be sure it will yield a permanent benefit.

That the hearty welcome which we have given you, our *ransomed* kinsmen, may be rendered a blessing, and that the advices which we have tendered may be as good seed sown in good ground, we shall continue to make supplications, prayers, intercessions and thanksgivings to Him whose care reaches all, because His love embraces all.

To Him we commend you, O ye who are now as sheep without a shepherd—as *exiles in the land of your nativity*.

May He who led Abraham, Isaac and Jacob, as they wandered over Canaan and Egypt, guide, protect and bless you; raise up kind, influential friends to do you good; and when the purposes of his grace shall have been accomplished in you, may you be able, like Jacob, to say: "With my staff I passed over this Jordan, and now I am become two bands."

Now, if we ask, who has sent us this great deliverance? The answer shall be, the Lord; the Lord God Almighty, the God of Abraham and Isaac and Jacob.

But as He blessed the chosen seed, by the ministry of men and angels, so in our case, the angels of mercy, justice and liberty, hovering over the towering Capitol, inspired the heads and hearts of the noble men who have plead the cause of the poor, the needy and enslaved, in the Senate and House of Representatives.

For the oppressed and enslaved of all peoples, God has raised up, and will continue to raise up, his Moses and Aaron. Sometimes the hand of the Lord is so signally displayed that Moses and Aaron are not recognized. Seldom do they recognize themselves.

There was neither bow, spear, nor shield, in the hand of Israel, when the Lord led him forth from Egypt, so also, there was no weapon of offence nor defence in your hands when this *ransom* was brought you.

"Great and marvelous are thy works, Lord God Almighty, just and true are thy ways, thou King of Saints. Who shall not fear thee, O Lord, and glorify thy name? We praise thee, we bless thee, we worship thee, we glorify thee, we give thanks to thee for thy great glory. O Lord God, Heavenly King, God the Father Almighty."

Thou, O Lord, and thou alone couldst have moved the heart of this Nation to have done so great a deed for this weak, despised and needy people!

We will, therefore, make supplications, prayers, intercessions, and thanksgivings, for "All that are in authority."

The duty of supplications in behalf of the Government is rendered more binding upon us, when we consider the circumstances under which it was written. St. Paul lived under the reign of Nero, the bloody emperor, who having set Rome on fire, amused himself with drinking and music while the city was in flames; and afterwards, accused the Christians of the crime which he himself had committed, thereby causing many of them to be put to death in the most cruel manner.

Now, if it was the duty of the ancient Christians to pray for such monsters of wickedness, by how much more is it our duty to pray for a Christian Government.

Congress need our supplications, they shall have them. The President and his Cabinet need our prayers, they shall possess them. The Supreme Court, that awful emblem of impartial justice, need our intercessions, it shall not be forgotten.

Upon all these departments of law, authority and power, we shall beseech the God of Nations to send the spirit of wisdom, justice, liberty —of wisdom seeing the end from the beginning— of justice incorruptible—of liberty governed by righteous law.

To make supplications, prayers, intercessions, and thanksgiving for these authorities, is the peculiar privilege of the Colored People in the United States.

They are not permitted, as in the days of the Revolution and the war of 1812, to take up arms in defence of the Government. Some, both among Anglo-Saxons and Anglo-Africans, complain of this prohibition. For my part, I am glad of it, because I think I see the hand of God in it.

The present war is a kind of family quarrel. Therefore, let a stranger take heed how he meddles, lest both parties unite to drive him out of the house. "Why shouldst thou meddle to thy hurt?"

But we can wield a power in behalf of the Government which neither rifled cannon, nor mortar, nor rocket-battery can assail, nor bomb-proof walls resist.

That power is the right arm of God—of God, who lifts up and casts down nations according as they obey, or disregard the principles of truth, justice, liberty.

The service of prayer which is required from us, contemplates the most difficult as well as the noblest objects. It contemplates the end of the war. It contemplates legislation before and after the end.

Now, to manage this war, so as to bring permanent good to all concerned, requires more than human wisdom—more than human power. To legislate so as to make the masses see and feel that the laws are just, wise, beneficial, demand more than human learning or skill in government. To determine the sense and just application of these laws as Judges—to execute them faithfully and impartially as a Chief Magistrate, O how much of the spirit of God is needful! How much in the President! how much in his Cabinet!

Then there is the army. Let us not forget the brave men who constitute it—who have left their comfortable homes, beloved families, fond parents, affectionate sisters and brothers, for the hardships, dangers and painful deaths of the battle field.

Let us pray that, as *some of them are,* so *all may become,* soldiers of the Cross; so that such as are doomed to fall in the fight, may rise from their gory beds to obtain a crown of life;

and those who may return to the peaceful pursuits of civil life, may be wiser and better men.

Now, then, although weak, few, despised and persecuted, we can aid all these departments of government by our daily supplications, prayers and intercessions.

In doing this service, we can accomplish what we could not if we were leading the van of battle; for conquering armies are preceded and succeeded by anguish, misery and death, but our service brings down nothing but blessings upon all.

They are also weapons, "not carnal, but mighty through God, to the pulling down of strongholds;" even the casting down of principalities and powers—the moving of heaven and earth.

Take two examples: When Israel fought against the five kings of the Amorites, Joshua prayed and the sun stood still upon Gibeon, while the moon hung over the valley of Ajalon, till Israel had conquered.

"John Knox was a man famous for his power in prayer, so that Queen Mary used to say she feared his prayers more than all the armies of Europe. And events showed she had reason to do it. He used to be in such an agony for the deliverance of his country that he could not sleep. He had a place in his garden, where he used to go to pray. One night he and several friends were praying together, and as they prayed Knox spoke and said that deliverance had come. He could not tell what had happened, but he felt that something had taken place, for God had heard their prayers. What was it? Why the next news they heard was: 'Queen Mary is dead!'"

But the motives for all this work of mercy, faith, and love as furnished by the text are as weighty as they are numerous. 1st. "That we may lead a quiet and peaceable life." Peace and quietude are some of the conditions of happiness. Dr. Adam Bluche says: "If the State be not in safety, the individual cannot be secure; self preservation, therefore, should lead men to pray for the government under which they live. Rebellions and insurrections seldom terminate even in political good—and even where the government is radically bad, revolutions are most precarious and hazardous. They who wish such commotions would not be quiet under the most mild and benevolent government." This is true of communities and nations, as well as of individuals. We all desire it, and therefore it is our duty to labor for it by every instrument which Infinite wisdom has ordained and man can employ. And lo! how excellent the instruments! *Prayers, supplications, intercessions*—thanksgiving. As Aaron approached the Mercy Seat, with the smoking censor, and was accepted, so do we approach the throne of the Eternal with the burning incense of heaven's own making, and will be accepted. O, let us supplicate God for the peace and quietude of the whole nation!

2d. The other motive which Inspiration presents is, that we may live *"in all godliness* and *honesty."* Godliness first, honesty afterwards. The latter is the fruit of the former. The godly man, is he who fears God and keeps his commandments. Such a man will be honest in words as well as in deeds; in matters of truth as well as in matters of property. *Honesty is the only policy of godliness.* Colored men, write this sentiment upon your hearts, engrave it in your memory. Let all your thoughts, words, actions, be controled by this principle, *it is always safe to be honest, as it is always safe to be godly.* One has said, that "An honest man is the noblest work of God." But whence comes the honest man? Does he not spring out of the godly? Most assuredly. For no man is truly honest, uniformly honest, and universally honest, but he who is godly. Therefore be godly, and you will be honest in all things, at all times, in all places.

3d. The third motive for this heavenly duty, this intercession in behalf of the Government is, that "It is good and acceptable in the sight of God our Saviour." Whatever God accepts and pronounces good, *must be good:* good in itself; good in its effects, always good; good for man, because ordained of God.

4th. The last motive we present for this godlike work is, that God *"Will have all men to be saved, and to come unto the knowledge of the truth."*

Hence, we must pray for these Authorities not as public men only, but as private individuals also,—not as Chieftains of the Nation only, but as heads of families also,—as husbands, fathers, Christians. So that, while they think, write, speak, act for the public weal, their own souls may be brought under the saving power of the Gospel, and with all the members of their respective families be made the heirs of the grace of life.

O, that God may bring them all to the knowledge of the truth as it is in Christ Jesus! O, that every one of these Authorities may become a holy, wise, and just man! Then will the laws be enacted in righteousness and executed in the fear of the Lord.

These motives are enforced upon our considerations by the glorious example of the Lord Jesus Christ,* who is the Mediator between God and Man, who ever liveth to make intercession for his foes as well as his friends, and with whom there is no respéct of persons. Black men, red men, white men, are all alike before Him, and rise or fall, live or die as they please or offend Him.

To make prayers, intercessions, supplications, thanksgivings for national authorities you now clearly see *is a command from heaven.* Obey it, and you shall be blessed—always do it, and you shall be made a blessing to others. Whom God has blessed no man can curse. If God has blessed this nation, neither internal foes, nor foreign enemies can crush it.

But God will bless it if it will do right, administering justice to each and to all, protecting the weak as well as the strong, and throwing the broad wings of its power equally over men of every color. This is God-like, and God will bless

---

*When St. Cyprian defended himself befŏre the Roman Pro-Consul, he said, "We pray to God not only for ourselves but for all mankind, and particularly for the Emperors."

Tertullian in his Apology is more particular: "We pray for all the Emperors, that God may grant them long life, a secure government, a prosperous family, vigorous troops, a faithful senate, an obedient people; that the whole world may be in peace; and that God may grant both to Cæsar; and to every man, the accomplishment of their just desires."

So Ozigen: "We pray for kings and rulers, that with their royal authority they may be found possessing a wise and prudent mind."

See Dr. A. Clarke on the text.

his own image, be it in a nation or in a man. Then, O my country, "shall thy light break forth as the morning—thy health shall spring forth speedily—thy righteousness shall go before thee," and "the glory of the Lord shall be thy reward."

Then shall justice be engraven on our arms, and righteousness on our star-spangled banners; our armies shall then be led to battle by the Lord, and victory secured by the right arm of our God.

SERMONS

BISHOP DANIEL A. PAYNE, D.D., LL.D.

SERMONS

DELIVERED BY

Bishop DANIEL A. PAYNE, D.D., LL.D.,

BEFORE THE

General Conference of the A. M. E. Church,
INDIANAPOLIS, IND., MAY, 1888.

STENOGRAPHICALLY REPORTED.

EDITED BY
REV. C S. SMITH.

NASHVILLE, TENN.:
PUBLISHING HOUSE A. M. E. SUNDAY SCHOOL UNION.
1888.

EDITOR'S NOTE.

THE two sermons contained in this volume are the only sermons of Bishop Payne that have ever been published. It is true that fragments of other sermons of his may be found in print, but none save these in complete form. The fact that these sermons are the only ones delivered by Bishop Payne that have been published in full adds greatly to their value and significance. The sermons speak for themselves; and yet it is but just to say that much of their clearness and force is blurred and impaired by the inability of the stenographer, who is a foreigner of recent coming to this country, to preserve in character-form in every particular the exact words which constituted the utterances of Bishop Payne.

The sermons were not preached from manuscript, neither were they arranged in that form. They are the extempore sayings of a man full of years and wisdom. The sermons in published form by no means reveal the spirit in which they were delivered. If ever man spake with the "tongue of fire," it was Bishop Payne on the occasion of the delivery of these two sermons. Though weighted with the infirmities of more than seventy-seven years, he seemed to be as strong and vigorous as a young giant. That he spake under the in-

fluence of an inspiration there can be no doubt. He
was cognizant that for the last time he was lifting up
his voice in instruction, admonition, and exhortation
to the legislative body of the Church to whose upbuild-
ing and welfare he had devoted nearly fifty years of his
life; and it is evident that he had sought the divine
presence in frequent and earnest prayer. It is very
certain that the Spirit of God rested upon him. Much
that is said in the quadrennial sermon was anticipatory
of the ordination sermon. The first sermon will take
higher rank as an exegetical production; the second is
more glorious in that it graphically portrays the perfect
manhood of the despised Nazarene, and appeals to
man's highest consciousness to strive to imitate Him in
whom there was no guile.

THE QUADRENNIAL SERMON.

DELIVERED MAY 10, 1888.

Subject: "The priesthood of the Hebrew Church identical in character and design with the ministry of the Christian Church." *Text:* Malachi ii. 4–7.

WE come this morning, brethren, according to appointment, to deliver the quadrennial discourse. Of course our theme will be addressed particularly to the ministers before us—those of the A. M. E. Church, who represent the Church as a whole.

We find our text recorded in Malachi ii. 4–7: "And ye shall know that I have sent this commandment unto you, that my covenant might be with Levi, saith the Lord of hosts. My covenant was with him of life and peace; and I gave them to him for the fear wherewith he feared me, and was afraid before my name. The law of truth was in his mouth, and iniquity was not found in his

(5)

lips: he walked with me in peace and equity, and did turn many away from iniquity. For the priest's lips should keep knowledge, and they should seek the law at his mouth: for he is the messenger of the Lord of hosts."

I shall also read the following passages: "Behold, I will send my messenger, and he shall prepare the way before me: and the Lord, whom ye seek, shall suddenly come to his temple, even the messenger of the covenant, whom ye delight in: behold, he shall come, saith the Lord of hosts. But who may abide the day of his coming? and who shall stand when he appeareth? for he is like a refiner's fire, and like fullers' soap. And he shall sit as a refiner and purifier of silver: and he shall purify the sons of Levi, and purge them as gold and silver, that they may offer unto the Lord an offering in righteousness. Then shall the offering of Judah and Jerusalem be pleasant unto the Lord, as in the days of old, and as in former years. And I will come near to you to judgment; and I will be a swift witness against the sorcerers, and against the adulterers, and against false swearers, and against those that oppress the hireling in his wages, the widow, and the fatherless, and that turn aside the stranger from his right, and fear not me, saith the Lord of hosts." (Mal. iii. 1–5.)

"And of Levi he said, Let thy Thummim and thy Urim be with thy holy one, whom thou didst prove at Massah, and with whom thou didst strive at the waters of Meribah; who said unto his father and to his mother, I have not seen him; neither did he acknowledge his brethren, nor knew his own children: for they have observed thy word, and kept thy covenant. They shall teach Jacob thy judgments, and Israel thy law: they shall put incense before thee, and whole burnt sacrifice upon thine altar. Bless, Lord, his substance, and accept the work of his hands: smite through the loins of them that rise against him, and of them that hate him, that they rise not again." (Deut. xxxiii. 8–11.)

"This is a true saying, If a man desire

the office of a bishop, he desireth a good
work. A bishop then must be blameless,
the husband of one wife, vigilant, sober, of
good behavior, given to hospitality, apt to
teach; not given to wine, no striker, not
greedy of filthy lucre; but patient, not a
brawler, not covetous; one that ruleth well
his own house, having his children in sub-
jection with all gravity; (for if a man know
not how to rule his own house, how shall he
take care of the Church of God?) not a novice, lest being lifted up with pride he fall
into the condemnation of the devil. Moreover he must have a good report of them
which are without; lest he fall into reproach
and the snare of the devil." (1 Tim. iii. 1–7.)

"Let no man despise thy youth; but be
thou an example of the believers, in word,
in conversation, in charity, in spirit, in faith,
in purity." (1 Tim. iv. 12.)

We begin our discourse by asking: Of
what is the Christian Church composed?
We reply: It is composed of all true believers, so that every man and every woman who

has been fully consecrated to the Lord Jesus
Christ is a part of the Christian Church.
Indeed, collectively these constitute the spiritual temple, the Church, the family, so
called by the Apostle Paul, which is built
up of living stones into the spiritual temple.
Each man and each woman is a living stone
of which this temple is constructed. God
himself lives in this temple; he moves in
this temple; he works in this temple. He
lives, works, and moves in this temple by
a direct agency, which is called the Com-
forter—the spirit of holiness and the spirit
of truth. Co-operating with this direct agency are consecrated men, who are in part
called bishops, priests, and deacons. They
are called, or form, the Christian ministry.
Of old it was the Hebrew priesthood, now it
is the Christian ministry. The Church has
existed in all ages and amongst all nations.
As indicated in the book of Genesis, Enoch
was the visible head of the temple. He was
always walking with God and preaching
righteousness. The Church was founded in

the ark, the visible head of which was Noah.
When they came out of the ark the persons
representing the Church were eight—Noah,
his three sons (Shem, Ham, and Japheth),
and their families. Each of these three sons
was at the head of a family, and from them
came the patriarchs and priests of God.
God seemed to have chosen Shem for the
purpose of revealing to him his will concerning all the families of the earth, to make
known to the Shemitic branch of the sons
of Noah what he intended to do. This dis-
tinction came to Shem, the patriarch, and it
descended from patriarch to patriarch until
we come to Abraham, who was found at the
head of the visible Church of the living God.
The patriarch Abraham transmitted it to his
son Isaac, and Isaac to Jacob, and he to his
twelve sons. The third son of Jacob was
Levi, who seemed to have been remarkable
for his zeal and for his love of Korah; and
so great was his burning zeal for that which
was pure that it caused him to draw the
sword and slay the seducer of his sister Di-

nah, and he consecrated himself by that very
act to be the head of the house. We find
the same burning zeal breaking out at Mount
Sinai, while Moses was receiving instructions
of God concerning the Church which he was
now about to institute as typical of the coming glory of the Christian Church. God
told him to go down, because the people
were corrupting themselves. And as Moses
descended with Joshua they heard the children of Israel shouting, and Joshua said, "It
is the noise of war;" but Moses said, "No;
it is the shout of those that seem to be joyous." So they went down, and found Aaron,
a man chosen of God to be a priest, leading
the people astray to worship a golden calf.
And when Moses saw it he was shocked, for
he was a Levite, and he threw the tables of
stone which God had given him on the
ground and broke them, and Moses's indignation burned against Aaron. So Moses
stood in the gate of the camp with the people around him, and said: "Let those who
are on the Lord's side come unto me." And

the sons of Levi rushed to his side, and he
said: "Let every man gird his sword upon his
thigh, and consecrate himself, and go in and
out from gate to gate throughout the camp,
and slay every man his neighbor." That
was the second consecration of Levi to God's
service. Another one is recorded in the
book of Numbers. It so happened that as
the children of Israel were passing through
a waste, howling wilderness to the promised
land they came in contact with the Moabites
and the Midianites, who were not only an
idolatrous but also an adulterous people, with
whom the masses of the Israelites became
corrupted, and it seems so thoroughly corrupted that one of them, by name Zimri, the
son of Salu, a prince of a chief house among
the Simeonites, in open daylight and in the
presence "of Moses and in the sight of all
the congregation of Israel," took a Midian-
itish woman into his tent for adulterous purposes. And when Phinehas, the son of Eleazar, the son of Aaron, saw it, he rose up
from among the congregation, and took a

javelin in his hand, and he went after Zimri, and thrust both of them through their entire bodies; and the anger of the Lord was appeased, for his indignation waxed so hot against the adulterous conduct of the Israelites that twenty-four thousand of them died in a single day. And by this holy, burning zeal of Phinehas the Levites dedicated themselves the third time, and so this was the third time that the Lord consecrated them unto himself, and gave to Phinehas, and to his house, and to his seed after him "the covenant of an everlasting priesthood, because he was zealous for his God, and made atonement for the children of Israel." So much for the origin of the consecrated house of Levi.

Now I want to show to you, my dear brethren, that that same character which God demands in the Levitical priesthood he also demands in the Christian ministry. To unfold this character is now our work. We find the elements of this in the second chapter of the prophecy of Malachi. As you will remember, Malachi was the last of the prophets, and from him we have the condition of the Jewish Church and State at that time. Now the same laws which governed the State governed the Church. God was at the head of the Church and the State, and those who were governors or judges held their appointments of God. Now the Hebrew Church and State were corrupt, and God sent Malachi with this message to the priests and people: "And ye shall know that I have sent this commandment unto you, that my covenant might be with Levi, saith the Lord of hosts. My covenant was with him of life and peace; and I gave them to him for the fear wherewith he feared me, and was afraid before my name. The law of truth was in his mouth, and iniquity was not found in his lips: he walked with me in peace and equity, and did turn many away from iniquity. For the priest's lips should keep knowledge, and they should seek the law at his mouth: for he is the messenger of the Lord of hosts." (Mal. ii. 4–7.) In this statement we have the elements of the character of Levi represented in the direct priesthood. And now what is the first element in his character? Reverence for God. Fear means reverence, and so we shall strike out the word fear and use the word reverence. It was not the brutal fear which the child or man has for a cross dog or a woman for a drunken husband, because the man becomes brutish and the wife fears him as she would a lion or tiger. Not superstitious fear of hobgoblins, ghosts, and hags. That would have been disgraceful for such a man as Levi. Then what is meant by the word fear? Why, reverence for God and for his character, for his laws, for his commandments, for his statutes, and for his judgments. And this fear or reverence of Levi came from the highest love for the infinite God of Israel—the pure and spotless God. All the elements of God—holiness, righteousness, mercy, and justice and truth, and all the other attributes, which I need not name—were revealed by him to the prophets and patri-

archs. The instructions which were given
to Moses on Mount Sinai dealt with the
moral law, the civil law, and the ceremonial
law. We have three or four forms of law
given to God's people on Mount Sinai by
the Lord. And you will remember, my
dear children, that all these forms of law
were for the regulation of God's people in
Church and State. With the civil enact-
ments were statutes showing the moral law,
which formed the statutes of the living God
from that time to the present. They have
always shown that they are, without excep-
tion, suited to the Church of God and the
State. It was so in the days of Moses and
Aaron, and is even so now. Nothing con-
flicts with the law, and every thing, to be
right, must be in conformity with the divine
law. Now God made himself known to
Levi as good, holy, true, merciful, just, and
great, and every thing that makes up not a
god, but the Almighty God. He was so conscious of God's greatness and goodness and
of the majesty of his laws that he bowed be-

fore the commandments of the Lord. He
had a true sense of God's commandments for
priests. He moved as an archangel before
the throne of God, and the fear of God was
always upon his eyes and heart.

He is the Lord of truthfulness and veracity. Another of the elements of Levi's
character is this: he was blessed under the
covenant of Levi, and peace was given him.
Unto him was given life in all its aspects, in
its moral form, social form, and ethical form.
He was given peace, so that he was the embodiment of equity. There was no deception in his lips, no lie in any possible form,
no suppression of the truth when the truth
needed to be told, no prevarication or equiv-
ocation. Nothing that was possible to deceive the human intellect was to be found in
him, neither was it possible in the mouth or
on the lips of the messenger of the Lord.
Truthfulness and veracity were one of the
elements of the Levitical priesthood.

Holiness was another of the elements
of Levi's character, and this was expressed

2

in the statement, "He walked with me in
truth and equity." No man can walk with
God unless he is a holy man. "Can two
walk together," saith Amos, "unless they
are agreed?" Can a man who loves temperance keep company with a drunkard? He
may go into the company of intemperate
men, and labor to take one from among
them, but they cannot associate. The one
loves rum, and the other sobriety. But
where two men love temperance they can
walk together. You cannot find an honest
man in the company of a gambler, because
a gambler is a thief. They cannot agree;
there can be no sympathy between them.
And when we are assured that Enoch walked
with God we are also informed that he was
daily in communication with God in his
spirit, soul, and body—talking with God,
God talking with him. He was in sympathy
with God, God was in sympathy with him;
breathing the spirit of holiness, and the God
of holiness breathing the holy spirit on him.
And so when we read in the chapter before

us that Levi walked with God, and God gives
testimony concerning him, we must know
that he was a holy man; but when he had
corrupted the people by his ungodly living
it was difficult to turn him back to his pris-
tine condition, and therefore when we are
told that Levi walked with God—and God
does say so in the inspired words of Malachi—we must know that it angered God
when Levi deceived his Maker. We find
several things laid against Levi. The very
first charge against him is contained in the
general statement that he deceived the Lord,
and then comes the other statements of his
corrupting the temple of the living God. He
had violated the law of the living God, and
became abominable in the sight of the Lord.
There are terrible charges against him. Another charge against him was that he set
brother against brother and friend against
friend. He was accused of infidelity against
the wife of his youth and bosom. The character of his wickedness assumes three forms:
First, of corrupting the law; second, of caus-

ing the law to be a stumbling-block to the
people; and third, of telling the people that
evil was good in the sight of the Lord. O
what a terrible form of corruption Levi had
fallen into! The charge was brought by the
lips of Malachi to Levi to bring him back to
God. So, then, these are the elements of
the holiness of the character of Levi: he
walked with God, and when walking with
God he turned many to the Father and was
himself turned; he turned from his iniquity,
and the people followed him into the paths
of righteousness; he turned from sin and
walked in the paths of righteousness, and
the people followed him. Like priest, like
people. Holiness, we say, was one of the
elements of the character of Levi—uncom-
promising holiness, no tampering with sin
or iniquity. The unsheathed two-edged
sword was always in his hand, and was cast
against every thing that was set up against
the living God.

Then knowledge was another of the elements of Levi's character. But what was

it? Science? No. Literature? No. Philosophy? No. What then? The knowledge of the infinite God—that knowledge that telleth that God made man in his own image and after his own likeness. He had to make himself familiar with the forms of divine knowledge; he had to deliver God's message to his people in God's house. He studied by night and by day. He read, and became more and more familiar with the law and commandments of God. Science, literature, and philosophy were only secondary, and if at all resorted to were used only to make him better comprehend the law of the Lord and to speak the more successfully to the Lord's people. He was the messenger of the Lord of hosts, and the people had to go to him for instruction. Now how did he get the knowledge of the law? He studied God's book. He had before him then what we have now. He had not with him then what we have now. He had but the five books of Moses, and every Levite was bound by his vows to make them his daily

study. He was to get them in his brain,
then engrave them on his heart, and then
to let them out from his mouth as water
from the fountain. So did Levi live in the
light—in the light of God s truth and love—
and the people were always properly instructed. No matter what the question may
have been, he always answered. The teaching of the books was in his head and heart
and on his lips, so thoroughly was he familiar with the law of the living God. Now
such a man would be fit to be a messenger
of the Lord of hosts. Such were the requirements of the Almighty God of the Levitical priesthood.

The requirement now is that the character
of the people should be reformed. But this
is always a difficult task, because the *rox
populi* is always against God. The *rox populi*
nailed Jesus to the cross, but, as Paul says,
the Church of the living God still exists
and continues to do invaluable good. Now,
brethren, it is a very hard thing to bring
about reformation in a corrupt community

of men and women, be that community a
village, or a large town, or a great city like
New York or London, including four millions of living souls. It would be a very
difficult thing to reform such a community
—every thing tends for the worst. It is only
the messenger of the Lord who dares rebuke
the corrupt priests and people. He must go
to reform a corrupt people and priesthood.

We come now to the third part of our
text. Hear what Malachi says in the third
chapter: "Behold, I will send my messenger." And he did come when John appeared
on the banks of the Jordan. He was ready
for his work as a messenger of his coming.
Malachi goes on: "But who may abide the
day of his coming? and who shall stand
when he appeareth? for he is like a refiner's·
fire, and like fullers' soap: and he shall sit
as a refiner and purifier of silver: and he
shall purify the sons of Levi, and purge
them as gold and silver, that they may offer
unto the Lord an offering in righteousness."
Now, you know what fire does—it consumes

stubble. Every combustible thing will be consumed, and every dirty thing must be washed with water. Jesus came as a purifying fire to reform and to purge him of his guilt, that he may offer unto the Lord an offering in righteousness. He shall sit in the church or temple all the time. He is in the heart now. He is here working and purifying every thing in his grand and glorious house. But it sometimes happens in the act of purifying with fire that not only the dross is burned up, but also the pure and burnished gold which sticks too close to the dross. He came for the purpose of purifying, and he has sent me this morning to sound the warning. "He shall sit as a refiner and purifier of silver: and he shall purify the sons of Levi, and purge them as gold and silver, that they may offer unto the Lord an offering in righteousness."

Now we come to finish our view on the character of the Levitical priesthood. Its design and purposes are indicated in the chapter which I have read to you. Salva-

tion was the end of the Levitical priesthood
—to make the living God known, to make
known the I AM in all the ways possible for
man to know him. The priesthood was instituted for that purpose—that the people
might learn to obey God, to love him, and to
love and respect his Church. Salvation was
the design of the Levitical priesthood.

Now we come to show you that the Christian ministry is identical with the Levitical
priesthood, and that it has the same design,
as will be seen from the first chapter of the
first book of Timothy. I do this in order
to help every brother before me who is a
Biblical student, and who makes the word
of God his daily study to gain a better
knowledge of God and be strengthened, for
he only is the man who comprehends this
grand and glorious thing—the character of
the Christian ministry and the design of
that ministry. Now remember, if you please,
that it was the Prophet Malachi who delivered God's message to Levi and to the people to whom Levi was sent. But here comes

a greater man than any Jewish priest—a
man caught up into the third heaven to be
instructed, to know things hitherto unut-
tered by human lips. Paul was above Moses,
far above the light which he pours upon the
human mind for all the ages and periods to
come—the man most like the God-man.
No man was so like Christ Jesus as was St.
Paul, and he was sent and commissioned by
the Lord Jesus Christ, the Lord of life, to
teach the Christian Church what Malachi
taught the Hebrew Church.

We now come to the third chapter of the
same Epistle. "This is a true saying, If a
man desire the office of a bishop, he desireth
a good work. A bishop then must be blameless, the husband of one wife, vigilant, sober,
of good behavior, given to hospitality, apt to
teach; not given to wine, no striker, not
greedy of filthy lucre; but patient, not a
brawler, not covetous; one that ruleth well
his own house, having his children in sub-
jection with all gravity; (for if a man know
not how to rule his own house, how shall he

take care of the Church of God?) not a novice, lest being lifted up with pride he fall
into the condemnation of the devil. Moreover he must have a good report of them
which are without; lest he fall into reproach
and the snare of the devil." Well, it is
said that no man should seek such an office.
No man would take such an office in the
days of the apostles, because it was danger-
ous. Every man who likes the office of a
bishop must be like St. Paul. He must pass
through persecutions, must be prepared to
be struck thirty-nine lashes on his bare
back; he must be hungry, thirsty, almost
naked; he must count all things dross but
the excellency of Jesus Christ. That was
the position of a bishop in those days. Hence
Dr. Clarke says in effect that the spirit which
now actuates men for the office was the glory
in the name bishop, its honor, and its title.
But there was no honor attached to it in the
days of the Apostle Paul. It was all strokes
and persecution. Paul worked with his
hands while he preached. But now a cer-

tain glory surrounds the office.   Men covet the D.D., LL.D.   It carries with it power and a name, and hence many desire it for its title, its honor, and its emoluments.

We come now to see what are the elements that compose the licentiates, deacons, and elders of the Church of God, from the latter of whom the bishops are taken.   Before you can be a bishop you must be a licentiate, next a deacon, then an elder, and then comes the setting aside to the bishopric.   The elements of a bishop must therefore be many.   Let us look at them.   He must be blameless, without reproach; he must be the embodiment of holiness and truth, because his object is to save sinners.   He must not turn backward, he must examine all his steps, he must be the most blameless man in the community in which he lives; not guilty of any act of dishonesty, no cheat; nothing that is bad or impure must soil his history.   His character must manifest itself in his daily talk.   He must be a gentleman; he must not be a bigamist, nor must he love divorcement. If he divorces one wife and takes another woman to his bosom he is a reproach to the bishopric. He must be free from such blame. He must be vigilant, always watchful for the interest of the Church of the living God. He must be always looking out like a sentinel upon the summit of the citadel, calling the sleeping soldiers, that no enemy may take them by surprise. He must be watching on the right and watching on the left, like the man who has to guide a steam-boat down the St. James, and who is always looking out for the rocks on either side, that the boat may not strike against them and founder, and thereby lose the precious cargo. He must keep the Church pure and spotless as the bride of the Lord Jesus Christ; he must keep himself pure; he must be watchful; he must keep himself free from the stain of sin, as a shepherd of the flock, to prevent its being devoured by wolves; he must be sober. This does not only mean that he must keep himself free from the influence of liquor—he must be sober in pro-

nouncing judgment and in answering questions; he must look at questions which come
up for his decision from many sides. There
are many sides to a question. Some have
two, some three, some seven. Now, before
this man who stands at the head of Christ's
Church shall pronounce sentence in any
matter he shall first observe all sides of the
given question, so that his judgment may
be sound. He must not be half cracked in
the brain, not wanting in experience, but
spiritual minded, teaching the Christian the
way of the Lord. He should think rightly,
spiritually, justly. He must be a gentleman
—not rude, not crude, not given to passions.
Such men disgrace the Christian ministry,
and especially the bishopric. He must be
gentlemanly in his deportment at home and
abroad, in private and in public, representing the Lord Jesus Christ, who was the most
perfect gentleman that ever trod the earth.
He must be given to hospitality. He must
be always willing to give. Sometimes a man
is not able to give. Sometimes he is so poor

that he scarcely gets bread and butter for
his own family. Still he is willing to share
with the stranger according to his ability.
A minister should be liberal. A stingy man
is not worthy to be a preacher. He must be
liberal.

Then there are these two qualities which
ought to be possessed by every man, whether
he be licentiate, deacon, elder, or bishop:
He must have the capacity to take in knowledge as a sponge absorbs water, and must
make what he takes in a part of himself;
must be active, and have capacity to develop his activity. He must have a good
memory, and what he learns must be en-
graved on his heart; he must love it, live it,
and then give it out with his lips to the people. These are qualities which every man
who desires to be a minister should have:
He should in all things emulate the great
Teacher. He should be crucified to the world
and be dead unto sin, but alive unto righteousness through Jesus Christ our Lord.
He should be taught and instructed. He

should be holy, and then will come upon
him the Holy Ghost and the tongue of fire.
He should not be given to wine, but should
abstain from all forms of intemperance and
from every thing that intoxicates the brain.
No smoker of tobacco, no chewer of tobacco,
because tobacco deranges and impairs the
nervous system. He should abstain from
whisky, gin, rum, and brandy and all other
intoxicants. He should not be given to any
form of intemperance. He should be no
striker, nor given to fighting. He should
not be greedy of filth lucre. He should
not be a money-hog. It is always better
to give than to receive. No preacher who
is a money-hog should be made a bishop,
because he will do any thing to get money.
He will prevaricate, quibble, and do any thing
to obtain it, because it is his god. Such a
man is not fit for any office in the Christian
ministry. A minister should be patient
under persecutions, under trials, under temp-
tations—not brawling, barking, and biting
at every person who passes by, and some-

times barking at nothing. I have seen a dog bark and bark and bark at nothing, until one wondered that his throat did not get sore. Now, some men are like that, but such are not fit for the ministry.

A minister should not be covetous—coveting his brother's possessions. No such man is fit for the ministry. There is but one step from covetousness to idolatry. He should be one that ruleth well his own house, governing his wife and children—not allowing the boys to govern him and the girls to control their mother. The man who cannot teach and guide his house, his own province, is not fit to have charge of God's temple. He should know how to do this and that, and to put a stop to this and that, and to maintain discipline, and to say to the brethren, "This cannot be done," and if they persist, "Brethren, this shall not be done," and take the consequences. Never allow the brethren to violate the law; always stand by it, stand up and preach the living God. Never sacrifice justice to mercy nor mercy

3

to justice, but keep an equal balance between the two. The man who is all mercy will allow the truth to be perverted, and he that is all justice will become wicked—he will not spare. There must be a medium between the two. In purging the Church save all that can be saved. He should not be a novice. Put a man without experience, without knowledge in the leadership, and he is apt to become puffed up. If you, as we have said, put a man into authority, even as licentiate, before he is qualified for the position, you will make him get puffed up and beside himself; another thing, he will be apt to be ungovernable, so that neither bishop nor elder will be able to govern him.

Then he should have a good report of them which are without before he enters the ministry. We say this is a prerequisite. He should not have been a drunkard or a thief or a burglar. You may make a Christian of such a being, but if you make one a minister who is known to be guilty of either of these crimes, he will never be successful as a Christian minister. He cannot represent the Lord Jesus Christ. Make such a man a licentiate, deacon, elder, or bishop, and you disgrace the Church. You cannot find a single case in the Church's history where a drunkard or thief was ever taken into the ministry. God guards the Church against such as these. The idea which some have in regard to the thief on the cross is misleading and damaging. No man who has led such a life can be put into a holy office without dishonoring the Lord of hosts. Now I challenge any man here to give a single case in the Church's history in which such a man was ever made elder or bishop. No; he must be without reproach before he comes into the bishopric. A man who has not all the essential qualities for the office of bishop cannot be exalted to that position without disgracing the Church of the living God. He must have a good report. If we compare the two essential qualifications for the bishopric and the qualifications required of Levi, we will find that they are alike.

We shall now close by calling your attention to another qualification—humble-mindedness.   In the fourth chapter of First Timothy St. Paul says: "Let no man despise thy youth; but be thou an example of the believers, in word, in conversation, in charity, in Spirit, in faith, in purity." Be humble-minded, bear example to all believers, that they may imitate the Lord Jesus Christ.   A minister should be careful that the words coming from his lips be in harmony with the spirit of holiness.   His dealing ought to be in harmony with the Spirit of the living God as becomes a humble man and a teacher of the brethren, and this is the reason why I called upon my younger brethren to join me this morning in the opening service.   I wanted them to know that I have confidence in them.   There are young men in this house whom I can trust with all the interests of our Church, who are earnest and incorruptible— true in the midnight darkness and the midday brightness, true ever to Christ and the Church.   We have such men in the ministry, and I want them to know that I have confidence in them.

I shall now advert to my childhood for a few minutes. From my earliest childhood my mother taught me to reverence gray hairs. When a boy I was with my great-aunt at Charleston. There was in that city an old slave woman. I was taught to take off my hat and say "How d'ye do?" to every man and woman, and one day that old woman stopped me, asked my name, and said: "Why, you have such beautiful manners! God will bless you wherever you go, because you have beautiful manners." And my Uncle Daniel Bordeaux used to say to me: "My boy, respect every one that is older than yourself." I therefore know how to venerate gray hairs, and particularly in the Church, where they always indicate holiness and usefulness.

We have shown the semblance between the Levitical priesthood and the Christian ministry. We shall now show you the differences in the rites between them, because you can only thoroughly know the two by

comparing them. You cannot know the
two by merely finding out the points of resemblance, but also the points of difference;
and then, and then only, can you understand
the two. The Levitical priesthood was
marked by the most solemn vows and ceremonies. Do you want to know what they
are? It would take a day to tell them. The
most solemn ceremonies and plighted vows
they were. Please turn to the books of Exodus and Leviticus, where you will find them.
There was to be the bloody sacrifice of the
spotless lamb morning and evening; the
new-moon sacrifice once a month; then
there was the sacrifice of the bullock, upon
which Aaron and his sons pressed their
hands; then there was the offering up of the
two rams, whose blood was to be sprinkled
by the high-priest upon the altar; then there
was the anointing oil and the dress called
the holy garment. "Next to his flesh he was
to wear a coat made of embroidered linen,
with sleeves to it; this coat was to reach to
his feet. Over the linen coat he was to wear

a coat or robe of blue, that had no sleeves. Around the lower edge of this robe were to be hung pomegranates made of purple and blue and scarlet. Between the pomegranates were to be hung golden bells, and over the robe of blue he was to wear a third coat. It was to be shorter than the robe of blue, and, like it, was to have no sleeves, but was to be of different colors; it was called the ephod. On his breast he was to wear a breastplate which had twelve precious stones upon it; and also the miter for his head, with a plate of pure gold fastened to it." But, brethren, Daniel tells us in his prophecies that an angel was sent from heaven to tell him that these rites and ceremonies would come to an end, and as soon as the Messiah appeared there would be an end of the bloody sacrifices. The minister of the gospel must be a humble man, because he is of the everlasting priesthood. He must not be like the priests of old, wearing beautiful garments and jeweled breastp ates, but he should be clothed in the garments of righteousness and holi-

ness, with the spiritual garments which are
full of glory and beauty. That is the way
the great High-priest came. And when he
came to his dying hour upon the cross he
cried out: "It is finished." All rites and
ceremonies were swept away by that dying
cry. Yes, all rites were swept away, and
shortly after was fulfilled the prophecy concerning the destruction of the temple; for
Titus, with his legions, utterly demolished
Jerusalem and the site of that temple in
which bloody sacrifices were wont to be
made. Yes, my brethren, gone, gone, gone,
forever gone! Were those bloody rites,
were those embroidered garments restored
again? No, not in the Christian Church.
Paul lived out this idea; he did not wear a
white ephod to dignify his position; he did
not need an ephod at all. The gold, blue,
and scarlet he did not need; he did not need
any miter on his head, or golden crown; he
did not need any of them. He went in every-
day garments to preach the Lord Jesus Christ
crucified, to suffer for him, to be scourged,

and to die.   Here we find the Jewish priesthood differing from the Christian ministry.
When Christ died upon Calvary he forever
abolished the use of the things of old.   Now,
the idea of our holiness to the Lord—that is
according to the idea of the Christian priesthood, as required in the last book, uttered by the lips of the Prophet Malachi—
are holy hearts and holy, spiritual lives and
walking with God.   These are the most
beautiful garments a man can wear.   I speak
with the fear of God.   I would rather be the
meek Paul than the Pope of Rome or the
Archbishop of Canterbury.   Let me be like
the meek and lowly Jesus; let me suffer for
Christ as Paul did, and work for him, that I
may in the end be glorified by him.   O
may he write these words upon the hearts
of the young brethren, that they may live and
work for him!   Amen!

BENJAMIN W. ARNETT, D.D.   WESLEY J. GAINES, D.D.

BENJAMIN T. TANNER, D.D.   ABRAM GRANT, D.D.

In point of seniority, according to election, the new bishops
rank as follows: Wesley J. Gaines, Benjamin W. Arnett, Benjamin
T. Tanner, Abram Grant—elected May 19, 1888.

(42)

THE ORDINATION SERMON.

PREACHED MAY 24, 1888.

This sermon was delivered on the occasion of the ordination of W. J. Gaines, B. W. Arnett, B. T. Tanner, and Abram Grant to the bishopric.

MY theme this morning is the manhood of Jesus and the influence of that manhood upon the races and the nations of humanity. I shall not take a single verse or text as the foundation of my theme, as it is usual to do on all occasions like this; but, striking out a new pathway for myself, I shall take the first ten verses of the eleventh chapter of the prophecy of Isaiah to give form and color to my subject. "And there shall come forth a rod out of the stem of Jesse, and a Branch shall grow out of his roots: and the Spirit of the Lord shall rest upon him, the spirit of wisdom and understanding, the spirit of counsel and might, the spirit of knowledge and of the fear of the

(43)

Lord; and shall make him of quick understanding in the fear of the Lord: and he
shall not judge after the sight of his eyes,
neither reprove after the hearing of his ears:
but with righteousness shall he judge the
poor, and reprove with equity for the meek
of the earth: and he shall smite the earth
with the rod of his mouth, and with the
breath of his lips shall he slay the wicked.
And righteousness shall be the girdle of his
loins, and faithfulness the girdle of his reins.
The wolf also shall dwell with the lamb, and
the leopard shall lie down with the kid; and
the calf and the young lion and the fatling
together; and a little child shall lead them.
And the cow and the bear shall feed; their
young ones shall lie down together: and the
lion shall eat straw like the ox. And the
sucking child shall play on the hole of the
asp, and the weaned child shall put his hand
on the cockatrice' den. They shall not hurt
nor destroy in all my holy mountain: for
the earth shall be full of the knowledge of
the Lord, as the waters cover the sea. And
in that day there shall be a root of Jesse,

which shall stand for an ensign of the people; to it shall the Gentiles seek: and his rest shall be glorious."

The first verse of this remarkable prophecy teaches the genealogy of Jesus. He is a Branch from the root, from the stem of Jesse. It shows his genealogy and proclaims his humanity. And this leads us to talk about the manhood, the exalted manhood, of Jesus Christ. Now what constitutes the elements of this eminent personage, whose individual character is to mold, form, tint, hue, and color all the races, all the nations, all the governments of the earth, and to harmonize the conflicting elements of humanity? We have these elements. "The Spirit of the Lord shall rest upon him." This marks him as a spiritual minded man, in opposition to the carnal-minded man, and teaches that he was always spiritual minded in all his feelings, all his thoughts, all the activities of the intellect, all the emotions and affections of the heart, and in the movements of the will. This spirit was in perfect harmony and oneness with the spirit of the

Father. Now the character of this spirit
which always rested upon Jesus was the
spirit of wisdom and understanding. These
two accompanied him. They were not sep-
arated; they were links in a single chain—
wisdom and understanding. Not knowledge, for knowledge is not wisdom; not
simple science, for that is not wisdom; not
literature, for literature is not wisdom; not
philosophy, for philosophy is not wisdom.
What, then, is wisdom? It is the power,
the gift, the endowment to know how to
use knowledge when acquired, how to in-
terpret knowledge, how to apply knowledge,
how to use it, and how and when to forbear
using it. This is wisdom. It plans as God
plans, and executes as God executes. Knowledge is only an instrument in the hand of
wisdom, only the sword by which it fights
and conquers, only the mode in which this
thing and that thing and the other thing is
known as resembling or differing one from
another. Wisdom rises and towers as far
above learning and talent as the heaven
towers above the earth. What is under-

standing? It is that power by which the human intellect recognizes the height and the depth, the length and the breadth of that which it undertakes to conquer. In the case of Jesus understanding was intuitive. The very moment the thing appeared before him, like a flash of lightning his intellect passed through it and touched the top and the bottom of it; indeed, every extremity of the thing was comprehended at a glance, and he understood it. That is understanding, young men, which gives not only the power to investigate this thing and that thing, but also to comprehend this thing and that thing, to know its difference from other things and its relation to every thing else. That is understanding. It was perfect in the manhood of Jesus Christ.

Wisdom and understanding—these are a part of the elements of Christ's manhood. Another two are counsel and might. They are coupled together as other links in the golden chain of the manhood of Jesus. You will remember that Isaiah, in the ninth chapter, tells us that a child was born to Is-

rael, and a Son was given, and his name was
called Wonderful. This was the perfect title
of Jesus, and the other one was Counselor.
Now counsel differs altogether from advice
and instruction. Instruction comes from
teaching, as we teach the alphabet to a
child, and show its need and the difference
between vowels and consonants, and as we
teach him the sound of each vowel and its
quantity in itself and its relation to words,
and then its relation to sentences. This is
instruction. Advice is a different thing. A
young man comes to me, and he says:
"Why, Bishop Payne, I am in trouble. I
cannot ask advice of anybody but you.
Will you please give it?" I say: "Yes; I
will. What is your trouble?" He tells me,
and I advise him. Counsel goes beyond advice. It instructs first and advises after-
ward, and then guides the young man into
the path in which he should go, and must
go, if he conquers himself and conquers the
difficulties which stand in his way. That
is counsel. Now this quality in the man
Jesus was perfect—more perfect than it is in

the archangel Gabriel or Michael, who stood
before the throne of God. It was perfect in
itself, and we have many instances of this
given us by the evangelists Matthew, Mark,
Luke, and John. Any one who sought his
counsel got it, and if it was acted on the
recipient never went astray. His counsel
never errs, and the man who follows that
counsel cannot go astray, because he is
guided by unerring wisdom in that particular direction. I want the young brethren
to remember this. Let Jesus be your Teacher, your Guide, and your Counsel in every
question concerning duty and character.
Follow no one whose counsel contradicts
the counsel of the Lord Jesus Christ, whom
God has given as our Counsel, our Guide,
and our Patron.

And then again the spirit of might was
another element in Christ's manhood. But
what constitutes might? Not physical
might, for the horse has might, the ox has
might, any wild beast has might; the lion,
the tiger, the elephant all have might in
themselves. But this is not what is meant;

4

it is not this sort of might which constitutes one of the elements of Jesus. It is moral excellence and purity of thought, uncontaminated by filth and rot, moving among the impure as the archangel moves among them, uncontaminated and untainted. That is moral might and purity. It comes down from heaven only to save, not to be contaminated. Let us strive, then, to bring moral might up to its high and pure position. To this is attached spiritual might, for they are inseparable. The great strength of the moral might comes from the spiritual, and the great strength of the spiritual comes from the moral. You cannot separate them. The spiritual-minded man is a moral man, the moral-minded man is also spiritual minded, and as he becomes more moral he becomes more spiritual, and as he becomes more spiritual he grows more moral. The spiritual-minded man cannot be immoral, the moral man cannot be otherwise than spiritual minded; for he is spiritual first, next moral. The Spirit of God pervades his heart, guides him, and makes him right-minded.

But this power, we are told, Jesus possessed from his birth. In the second chapter of the Gospel of St. Luke we are informed that the Spirit of God rested upon him from his birth, and it remained with him until his death. From the cradle to the grave he was mighty in the Lord, and strong in the Lord and in the power of his might. The Apostle Paul, in his Epistle to the Ephesians, exhorts them to "be strong in the Lord and in the power of his might." Now what is the might of God's power? It is omnipotent. The strength of God is omnipotent. He is an omnipotent Being. He was guided by a mighty spirit. He was strong in the Lord. He had conquered himself and the world. Then comes another couple—the spirit of knowledge and of the fear of the Lord. These form other links in the golden chain of the manhood of Jesus—knowledge and the fear of the Lord. Knowledge is to know what we learn and see. We know the nature of a certain thing in its differences and in its distinctions, as differing from that thing and the other thing and how related to this thing and that thing. That is knowledge— nothing else but knowledge, worldly knowledge. But the knowledge of Jesus came to him through the fear of the Lord. He pursued his investigations not in the spirit of vanity and pride. He did not say: "I am better than my fellows. I know more than they do. God has given me higher gifts than they." No; he pursued all knowledge —science, literature, and philosophy—in the fear of the Lord and with reverence in the presence of the Lord. No; he was always the gentle Jesus, and after all what was he at that time, and what was he in the presence of the great Creator but a mere baby held up by the hand of his Father, guided and supported by the hand of his Father? and all that Jesus did was done with reverence to that God who is infinite. He pursued all things in the knowledge of the Lord. He eschewed wickedness. These things are characteristic of the manhood of the Son of God.

Now see the effect of this combination of

endowments. He was made quick to understand every thing, so that his intellect, when it came into play, was apt; and his sensibility, when moved around here or there, acted as quickly as a flash of lightning or the rays from the center of the sun. He was quick to comprehend, quick to understand, and quick to retain. All the powers of his soul and body were animated by the Spirit of the Lord, and therefore he did not judge according to the sight of the eyes, nor yet according to the hearing of the ears. That is man's judgment—erring man, sinful man. We poor creatures judge according to the sight of the eyes, and, as you know, the eyes deceive. Let every one in this house, every man and woman, cast their memories back to the scenes of their past career, and see how often they have been deceived by the eyes. Look carefully into every thing that comes before you, search it to its very core, be sure that you see what it is before you judge it. Christ did not judge by the hearing of the ears, for the ears deceive. A man comes and tells me this thing and that

thing. It is false; but, not knowing, I believe it. I must not judge from what I
heard from his lips. I must go behind his
statements, and see that those things which
he told me are facts, before I give credit to
them. Such was the manhood of Jesus.
He judged no man or thing from hearing
with his ears or seeing with his eyes; but,
having the knowledge of the secrets of the
heart and the thoughts of the heart, he could
judge aright. He never judged wrongly.
And so, brethren, do not judge by the sight
of the eyes or the hearing of the ears, and
then get your facts to discover that you
have judged wrongly. First get your facts,
find out what produced the effect, and then
judge. "But with righteousness shall he
judge the poor, and reprove with equity for
the meek of the earth: and he shall smite the
earth with the rod of his mouth, and with the
breath of his lips shall he slay the wicked."

These are the manifestations of the wonderful character of Jesus, of his wonderful
manhood. "He shall smite the earth with
the rod of his mouth, and with the breath

of his lips shall he slay the wicked." You
say that he is unmerciful. It is not true.
By saying this you slander him. He is merciful. "He shall smite the earth." Mercy
and judgment go together. "He shall slay
the wicked." He shall purify the earth,
and make humanity good. He it is whom
we ought all to follow. Young men, follow
the Lord Jesus Christ, develop your manhood as he did his, and then you will never
make a mistake—you will act as bishops of
his Church ought to act. Now look at this
wonderful statement about Christ's manhood. In my quadrennial sermon I alluded
to the garments which were worn by the
high-priests, and those of you who remember your reading of Exodus and Leviticus
will recollect that the high-priest wore two
garments—his under-garment, and then a
flowing robe which touched the floor; embroidered skirts, and golden bells between
the pomegranates, so that as he walked
about there was a beautiful tinkling musical
sound. That garment was also embroidered with gold thread and blue thread and

scarlet thread; and then he wore a breastplate upon his bosom, beautified with twelve
different kinds of precious stones. Then
there was the ephod, which was made of
white linen, and also embroidered with scarlet thread. He also wore upon his head a
jeweled cap, and then the crown of gold.
These were the decorations called the glories
of the body. But Jesus wanted no such
things. He did not run after toys. They
were given to Aaron and the Levites for
toys. Young men, do not hanker after
these or any such like toys.

We are further told that "righteousness
shall be the girdle of his loins, and faithfulness the girdle of his reins." Now what
are the girdles of Jesus? Righteousness
and faithfulness. These are the garments
of truth and beauty, and I want these young
brethren to gird themselves with these qualities. Let your loins be girded with righteousness, and your reins with faithfulness.
Now what is meant by the words righteousness and faithfulness? What a complex
word is righteousness! How full of beauty!

Yea, I may say how full of sublimity and grandeur! I shall not stop to analyze it, but I may say that it is composed of two words. It has all the moral virtues and all the Christian graces combined in one. These make up righteousness. Brethren, gird yourselves with all the moral virtues. Faithfulness means steadfastness, stability, reliability, uncorruptibility, immovability—if I may so say, unshakability—in the man. He must be true to his God first of all, and then, being true to his God, he will be true to every human being upon the face of the earth. Never pocket a cent belonging to the widow that ought to be in the widow's hand. That is unfaithfulness. Never do that if you wish God to bless you. Never retain the widow's dues for a single moment. Give to the fatherless and widow; always hasten to give her what is hers; never oppress her. If you would have God bless you and yours, never do these things. Be faithful to every trust given you, be it soever great or small. Always be faithful. Never break a promise. If you promise to give a man ten dollars to-morrow, give them to him if you have to stint yourself. If you promise to give the cause of Christ one hundred dollars, give it if you have to stint yourself, because your word must be of more value than your gold. Be faithful to every trust given you by man and God. Be what the glorious Redeemer was. Let Jesus Christ be your model, for remember that he was the most perfect man, and his manhood is more beautiful than the beauty of the archangels and more majestic than the majesty of the archangel Gabriel.

The glorious manhood of Jesus Christ is the only true type of real manhood. I pray thee, then, I beg you, to study it, study it, study it as your only model; study it, study it, study it until it penetrates your hearts and souls, and guides every movement of your hearts, wills, and intellects. Be like Jesus—the most perfect man that ever was or will be on this earth. Let your character be as beautiful as his was. Let his glorious virtues be in you, and make you like the archangels in heaven. God grant that every one of you may be so perfected!

Jesus Christ's manhood was a fact, for the prophet draws no imaginary picture. He predicted what did happen and what is yet to come. It is no mere history. The difference between history and prophecy is this: history records past events, prophecy predicts coming ones. Now the Prophet Isaiah prefigures to us what is to come and what will come to pass. He first says: "The wolf shall dwell with the lamb." What does that mean? Shall the wolf become a lamb? No such thing. Shall the lamb become a wolf? No. Why if you could amalgamate the lamb and the wolf, you would produce a monstrosity, which would have eight legs, four eyes, and two tails. It means that the two shall be harmonized; they shall dwell together, not become one. They shall dwell side by side; they shall dwell in harmony, but they will not be united. No; you cannot do that. It would be an utter impossibility. God never intended that. They will be harmonized, they will be fraternized, they shall be made to live in peace. This is emblemati

of the influence of the Lord Jesus Christ
upon all the races. "The leopard shall lie
down with the kid." They shall not become one, but shall sleep together, neighbor
and neighbor, in perfect harmony and peace.
That is the idea of the glorious prediction.
Then the prophet goes on to say: "The
calf and the young lion and the fatling shall
lie down together." They shall pasture in
the same pasture, feed in the same pasture
of thynne and clover, if you please; but the
one shall not bite the other, the one shall
not snarl at the other. Each shall be happy
in himself, and each shall try to make the
other happy. That is the idea of the passage. But there is yet another: "And the
cow and the bear shall feed; their young
ones shall lie down together; and the lion
shall eat straw like the ox." The lion shall
not become an ox, nor the ox a lion, but
they shall live in peace and harmony, in
perfect harmony one with the other. For
the lion, which is now disposed to eat the
calf, shall not then touch it; but the king
of the forest shall eat straw like the ox.

What beautiful pictures! And what is meant? Why this: that all races shall become harmonized, and live in peace; that war-loving nations, like England and Prussia, shall cease to fight. Germany shall not be at enmity with France, nor Italy with Spain. The different nationalities of Europe shall not continue to wage war against each other. The sword shall then be turned into a plowshare, and the spear into a pruning-hook. The time is coming, it is fast approaching, when all the nations of the earth shall harmonize and live in peace to make way for the second coming of the Son of man.

"And the sucking child shall play on the hole of the asp, and the weaned child shall put his hand on the cockatrice' den." The principle of that shall be recognized. It is but a picture of a fact which is to come in the future. Every thing shall be so harmonized that nothing shall disturb the harmony of the community of the Lord. What a community that shall be! Its glory shall never be destroyed, " for the earth shall be

full of the knowledge of the Lord, as the
waters cover the sea"—the knowledge of
God the Father, God the Son, God the Holy
Ghost, and God the Redeemer; not the
knowledge of man. No; a knowledge that
is greater than that—that kind of knowledge which comes of the gospel. Yes; the
gospel shall cover the earth as the waters
cover the sea. This is what you are to teach.
Do not try to set race against race. That is
the work of the devil, not of Christ. You
must not set the white man against the
black man, nor the brown man against the
yellow man; but harmonize them all, and
teach them to walk in peace. It is your
work to teach the gospel of the Lord Jesus
Christ—that he died for all. You must try
to save all, and make all live in one common
brotherhood.

And now we come to the next passage:
"And in that day there shall be a root of
Jesse, which shall stand for an ensign of the
people." Yes; it will be that glorious and
conquering name, that immortal name. St.
Paul says so, for he testifies that there is no

other name under heaven, given among
men, whereby men can be saved, but the
name of Jesus. But Isaiah proclaimed it
before St. Paul preached it. No other
name, my brethren, can conquer the globe
but the name of Jesus. All men should
seek that name. It shall conquer all differences between the peoples, and harmonize
all conflicting views, and make us go in
peace.

I have gotten through with my text, and
now allow me to say to you, as your senior,
get down on your knees, and wrestle until
the Lord Jesus Christ shall be in you. It is
said of a man who was naturally of an ex-
citable temperament, and who was very
easily angered, that he found out he could
not live as he ought to have lived until that
irritable temper was conquered; and so he
would fall upon the floor in agony, and
wrestle for victory over himself, and he ultimately succeeded in conquering his unruly
temper. Do not say, therefore, that unruly
dispositions cannot be conquered. I beg
you to follow this example, and struggle

with Christ until you are conformed in him. Hold on, and beg and wrestle with the angel, as Jacob did, until your name be changed from Jacob to Israel. Conquer the devil, conquer your temper and passions and vices. As for crime, I shall not talk about that. The minister of the Lord Jesus Christ does not know what crime is. Christ never committed a crime. He was sinless from birth to death, and as ministers you must be blameless. You cannot go down to the drunkard's den, the gambler's den, or the harlot's brothel. Live as though you were constantly in the presence of the eternal God. You will have power then, having conquered yourselves, to conquer the world, as the Lord Jesus did. Study him, study him as your model; study the perfect model of manhood until he shall be conformed in you. Finally, my brethren, I say to you in the words of St. Paul: "Be strong in the Lord, and in the power of his might." Amen, and amen.

Religion in America
Series II

An Arno Press Collection

Adler, Felix. **Creed and Deed:** A Series of Discourses. New York, 1877.

Alexander, Archibald. **Evidences of the Authenticity, Inspiration, and Canonical Authority of the Holy Scriptures.** Philadelphia, 1836.

Allen, Joseph Henry. **Our Liberal Movement in Theology:** Chiefly as Shown in Recollections of the History of Unitarianism in New England. 3rd edition. Boston, 1892.

American Temperance Society. **Permanent Temperance Documents of the American Temperance Society.** Boston, 1835.

American Tract Society. **The American Tract Society Documents,** 1824-1925. New York, 1972.

Bacon, Leonard. **The Genesis of the New England Churches.** New York, 1874.

Bartlett, S[amuel] C. **Historical Sketches of the Missions of the American Board.** New York, 1972.

Beecher, Lyman. **Lyman Beecher and the Reform of Society:** Four Sermons, 1804-1828. New York, 1972.

[Bishop, Isabella Lucy Bird.] **The Aspects of Religion in the United States of America.** London, 1859.

Bowden, James. **The History of the Society of Friends in America.** London, 1850, 1854. Two volumes in one.

Briggs, Charles Augustus. **Inaugural Address and Defense,** 1891-1893. New York, 1972.

Colwell, Stephen. **The Position of Christianity in the United States,** in Its Relations with Our Political Institutions, and Specially with Reference to Religious Instruction in the Public Schools. Philadelphia, 1854.

Dalcho, Frederick. **An Historical Account of the Protestant Episcopal Church, in South-Carolina,** from the First Settlement of the Province, to the War of the Revolution. Charleston, 1820.

Elliott, Walter. **The Life of Father Hecker.** New York, 1891.

Gibbons, James Cardinal. **A Retrospect of Fifty Years.** Baltimore, 1916. Two volumes in one.

Hammond, L[ily] H[ardy]. **Race and the South:** Two Studies, 1914-1922. New York, 1972.

Hayden, A[mos] S. **Early History of the Disciples in the Western Reserve, Ohio;** With Biographical Sketches of the Principal Agents in their Religious Movement. Cincinnati, 1875.

Hinke, William J., editor. **Life and Letters of the Rev. John Philip Boehm:** Founder of the Reformed Church in Pennsylvania, 1683-1749. Philadelphia, 1916.

Hopkins, Samuel. **A Treatise on the Millennium.** Boston, 1793.

Kallen, Horace M. **Judaism at Bay:** Essays Toward the Adjustment of Judaism to Modernity. New York, 1932.

Kreider, Harry Julius. **Lutheranism in Colonial New York.** New York, 1942.

Loughborough, J. N. **The Great Second Advent Movement:** Its Rise and Progress. Washington, 1905.

M'Clure, David and Elijah Parish. **Memoirs of the Rev. Eleazar Wheelock, D.D.** Newburyport, 1811.

McKinney, Richard I. **Religion in Higher Education Among Negroes.** New Haven, 1945.

Mayhew, Jonathan. **Observations on the Charter and Conduct of the Society for the Propagation of the Gospel in Foreign Parts;** Designed to Shew Their Non-conformity to Each Other. Boston, 1763.

Mott, John R. **The Evangelization of the World in this Generation.** New York, 1900.

Payne, Bishop Daniel A. **Sermons and Addresses,** 1853-1891. New York, 1972.

Phillips, C[harles] H. **The History of the Colored Methodist Episcopal Church in America:** Comprising Its Organization, Subsequent Development, and Present Status. Jackson, Tenn., 1898.

Reverend Elhanan Winchester: Biography and Letters. New York, 1972.

Riggs, Stephen R. **Tah-Koo Wah-Kan; Or, the Gospel Among the Dakotas.** Boston, 1869.

Rogers, Elder John. **The Biography of Eld. Barton Warren Stone, Written by Himself:** With Additions and Reflections. Cincinnati, 1847.

Booth-Tucker, Frederick. **The Salvation Army in America:** Selected Reports, 1899-1903. New York, 1972.

Satolli, Francis Archbishop. **Loyalty to Church and State.** Baltimore, 1895.

Schaff, Philip. **Church and State in the United States** or the American Idea of Religious Liberty and its Practical Effects with Official Documents. New York and London, 1888. (Reprinted from *Papers of the American Historical Association,* Vol. II, No. 4.)

Smith, Horace Wemyss. **Life and Correspondence of the Rev. William Smith, D.D.** Philadelphia, 1879, 1880. Two volumes in one.

Spalding, M[artin] J. **Sketches of the Early Catholic Missions of Kentucky;** From Their Commencement in 1787 to the Jubilee of 1826-7. Louisville, 1844.

Steiner, Bernard C., editor. **Rev. Thomas Bray:** His Life and Selected Works Relating to Maryland. Baltimore, 1901. (Reprinted from *Maryland Historical Society Fund Publication,* No. 37.)

To Win the West: Missionary Viewpoints, 1814-1815. New York, 1972.

Wayland, Francis and H. L. Wayland. **A Memoir of the Life and Labors of Francis Wayland, D.D., LL.D.** New York, 1867. Two volumes in one.

Willard, Frances E. **Woman and Temperance:** Or, the Work and Workers of the Woman's Christian Temperance Union. Hartford, 1883.